NIKOS KAZANTZAKIS
ODYSSEUS: A VERSE TRAGEDY

NIKOS KAZANTZAKIS

Odysseus:
A Verse Tragedy

Translation from the Modern Greek
And Introduction by
Kostas Myrsiades

SOMERSET HALL PRESS
Boston, Massachusetts

Odysseus, by Nikos Kazantzakis
© Copyright 2022 Niki Stavrou (all rights reserved throughout the world)
English Translation by Kostas Myrsiades

Published by Somerset Hall Press
416 Commonwealth Avenue, Suite 612
Boston, Massachusetts 02215
www.somersethallpress.com

ISBN: 978-1-935-244-25-7
E-book: 978-1-935-244-26-4

Cover image, contributed by Mikhail Hoika, used under license from Shutterstock.com.

LIBRARY OF CONGRESS CATALOGING-IN-PUBLICATION DATA

Names: Kazantzakis, Nikos, 1883-1957, author. | Myrsiades, Kostas, translator, writer of introduction.
Title: Odysseus : a verse tragedy / Nikos Kazantzakis ; translation from the Modern Greek and introduction by Kostas Myrsiades.
Other titles: Odyseia (Play) English
Description: Boston, Massachusetts : Somerset Hall Press, [2022] | Summary: "A tragic play about the Ancient Greek warrior-king Odysseus, and a prequel to Nikos Kazantzakis's epic poem The Odyssey: A Modern Sequel, inspired by Homer's The Odyssey"-- Provided by publisher.
Identifiers: LCCN 2022030575 (print) | LCCN 2022030576 (ebook) | ISBN 9781935244257 (paperback) | ISBN 9781935244264 (ebook)
Subjects: LCSH: Odysseus, King of Ithaca (Mythological character)--Drama. | LCGFT: Drama.
Classification: LCC PA5610.K39 O513 2022 (print) | LCC PA5610.K39 (ebook) | DDC 889.2/32--dc23/eng/20220705
LC record available at https://lccn.loc.gov/2022030575
LC ebook record available at https://lccn.loc.gov/2022030576

CONTENTS

Introduction, *by Kostas Myrsiades*   9

A Reading of Nikos Kazantzakis's Odysseus:
A Verse Tragedy, *by Kostas Myrsiades*   17

Nikos Kazantzakis's Odysseus:
A Verse Tragedy, *translation by Kostas Myrsiades*   49

About the Author   187

About the Translator   189

For Linda, Yani, and Leni

Beyond the rising wave, Ithaca comes in view ...

*True revolutions
are ignited by consenting minds
erupting spontaneously
whenever eye meets eye,
as when Penelope before the beggar caught Odysseus' eye.
"Stranger," she said,
"I shall decree a contest on this day.
One arrow must each suitor whip through twelve ax heads;
something only my lord can do."
The beggar relaxed his eyes.
"Let there be no postponement of this trial, Lady.
Death to the suitors; not one will escape his doom."
Their gazes touched once again
and both Odysseus and Penelope
knew.*

INTRODUCTION

Kostas Myrsiades

Nikos Kazantzakis (1883-1957), the modern Greek poet, novelist, essayist, and philosopher,[1] was throughout his professional writing career preoccupied with Homer's Odysseus. In 1922, he published his verse tragedy *Odysseus* in the Alexandrian periodical *Nea Zoe* under his pseudonym A. Geranos. The play was subsequently published in Athens in 1928 by the publisher Stokhastes and substantially revised and lengthened in a 1955 edition. In 1925, several years after completing *Odysseus*, the author began work on what he considered to be his crowning achievement, *The Odyssey*, an epic poem in 33,333 verses in a feminine (or double-rhymed) seventeen-syllable unrhymed iambic measure of eight beats. Kazantzakis labored through seven drafts of that work, finishing a sixth draft of 42,500 lines thirteen years later which he reduced to 33,333 verses in a seventh final draft and published under the title *The Odyssey* later that same year. In 1958, it was translated into English by Kimon Friar as *The Odyssey; A Modern Sequel* (hereafter referred to as *A Modern Sequel*). During this same period, 1932-1937,

Nikos Kazantzakis

Kazantzakis completed twenty-two cantos dedicated to people who had a significant role to play in his life and thought. The cantos, under the title *Tertsinas*, were written in Dante's triple rhyme, *terza rima*, the meter of the *Divine Comedy*. The author regarded these cantos as "bodyguards" of Homer's *Odyssey* and wanted to complete twenty-four in all, one for each of the *Odyssey* books but finished only twenty-two.

The tragedy *Odysseus* serves not only as a prequel to Kazantzakis's larger *A Modern Sequel* but also the vehicle that first introduced the versification used in that epic. The final two lines of the 1922 tragedy ("In my ponderous hands, death brings / peace like a thunderbolt in the hand of justice") segues smoothly into the first two lines of the author's 1938, twenty-four-part *A Modern Sequel* ("And when in his wide courtyards Odysseus had cut down / the insolent youth") as though he is continuing the narrative of *Odysseus* in the larger epic.

The two-part *Odysseus* can then be seen as a precursor to the over 800-page epic, although in the tragedy the character of Odysseus is still in an earlier stage of development. Odysseus's comment in Dante's *Inferno*, canto twenty-six, however, holds true for both the tragedy and the epic: "Neither fondness for my son, nor reverence for my aged father, nor due love that should have cheered Penelope could conquer in me the ardor that I had to gain experience of the world and of human vice and worth."[2] When Katzantzakis's Odysseus exclaims in *A Modern Sequel*, "My soul, your voyages have been your native land,"[3] it is as if he is responding to his host Eumaeus's question in the tragedy when

Odysseus: A Verse Tragedy

asked whether he is a native of Ithaca, "Which Ithaca? Be aware, old timer / a sailor counts the entire earth his home." Perhaps W.B. Stanford in his book *The Ulysses Theme* summarizes the main theme of both play and epic best: "Kazantzakis has singled out the wish to be free as the dominant passion of his hero."[4]

In an introduction to another play, *Sodom and Gomorrah*, Kazantzakis states that the purpose he set for all his dramatic works was to "reconcile the luminous and dark forces which exist in a state of war today, and attempt to divine the future harmony."[5] For him such harmony could be achieved in one of three ways. The first, which he rejects, is "the way of flight," to create romantic adventures in order to produce imaginary worlds. There, the reader can forget the difficult and dangerous reality of our epoch. The second, which he follows in his tragedy *Sodom and Gomorrah*, as well as in *Odysseus*, is "the way of disintegration." Here he attempts to illustrate the moral and spiritual anarchy of the world, which he sees crumbling before our eyes. The third way, "integration," however, was for him the best of the three in achieving future harmony because it was "the most upward striving"; but it was also the most dangerous. This is the way followed in *A Modern Sequel*; it can only be achieved by first passing through the "disintegration" level of *Odysseus*. Thereafter, the hero can attain the "integration" attempted in the epic.[6]

Kazantzakis's interest in Homer's Odysseus is manifested as early as 1914 after reading Gerhart Hauptmann's *Bow of Odysseus*, a play that deeply influenced his own. In a letter dated 9 August 1922 to his first wife

Nikos Kazantzakis

Galatea, Kazantzakis wrote that he intended to dedicate his tragedy to Hauptmann, but this never materialized.[7] In a second letter to his wife in 1923, he wrote, "I battle on, I look ahead like Odysseus, but I do not know whether I shall ever reach Ithaca. Unless the journey itself is Ithaca."[8] Kazantzakis was eager to see the tragedy published. In a number of letters to his friend and critic Pandelis Prevelakis, and to his publisher, he asked about its progress and expressed his desire to see it in print. In a letter dated 2 June 1928 he wrote to Prevelakis, "I am glad that *Odysseus* went to print; so you'll be in Athens to take care of him. I love him dearly, because after a long silence he broke out of my innards and—as the Scripture says—'ruptured the womb.'"[9] He pursued his obsession with *Odysseus* in his letters to Galatea and in a French translation he had completed which he was anxious to have put into verse.[10] Galatea's fondness for the tragedy filled the author with joy, "What you write me about my *Odysseus* sweetens my agony"[11]; "I found a French poet who is turning into verse for me the translation I had made of *Odysseus*."[12]

In the preface to *Nikos Kazantzakis and His Odyssey*, Prevelakis says, "I am certain that what a reader ultimately derives from [*A Modern Sequel*], as from *The Saviors of God*, is not nihilistic despair but the exaltation of life and man's fate," a comment that applies equally to the author's 1922 tragedy. Kazantzakis's Odysseus in both the tragedy and the epic is a rebel, uprooted, whose arena for action is the entire world. A solitary man who does not care for company, he is unlike Homer's hero, who finds peace in Ithaca. Kazantzakis's

Odysseus: A Verse Tragedy

hero is in search of god and ends up a killer of gods; he is a man of solitude, nostalgia, revolt, inhumanity, despair and nihilism. One of the main themes in Kazantzakis's two works is the search for an answer to "What is god?" (rather than "Who is god?") conflated with the question "What is freedom?" In both works, the essence of god is the attempt to find freedom and throw off the shackles that impede humanity's progress in the universe. The main difference between *Odysseus* and *A Modern Sequel* is that the earlier work was still concerned with human duality, the Apollonian rational self vs the Dionysian irrational self, whereas in the larger work, the hero reaches humanity's third dimension, the spirit or soul. In the tragedy, spirit and soul are still interchangeable with mind and intellect. It is not until the epic that Odysseus achieves a third dimension, a spiritual state, the state before ultimate nothingness.

Assessments of Kazantzakis's *Odysseus* have been favorably compared to the very work that inspired Kazantzakis to write it, Hauptmann's *The Bow of Odysseus*, written just eight years earlier.[13] Kazantzakis mirrors Hauptmann in several ways. Both works recreate Homer's *Odyssey*, books thirteen to twenty-two and conclude with the moment Odysseus is about to begin the slaughter of the suitors; they ignore the aftereffects of the killings related by Homer in books twenty-three and twenty-four. Kazantzakis sets the scene primarily before the swineherd Eumaeus's hut in the first part and at Odysseus's palace in the slightly shorter second part while Hauptmann's five act play is set at Eumaeus's hut in its entirety. In both tragedies, the action centers around the disguised Odysseus who returns to Ithaca to regain his kingdom, concealing his identity until the very end to expose his enemies and identify those who welcome his return. Similarly, the first part of each play deals with the beggar Odysseus interacting with household servants and the second with Penelope's suitors, using the main characters of Homer's epic: Odysseus, Telemachos, Penelope, Laertes, Eumaeus, Eurycleia, Melantho, and several suitors along with their leaders Antinoos and Eurymachos.

Kazantzakis departs significantly from Homer and Hauptmann however, not only in his handling of Penelope, who is all but ignored but also in his presentation of Odysseus, who is transformed into a rebellious Nietzschean superman unrecognized beneath his vagabond rags. Kazantzakis's character hints ironically at his true identity throughout, prevented by his larger-than-life persona from being taken as anything more than a braggart. His Odysseus is a man of mixed motives in a constant state of ethical tension always ready to take on even the gods if need be. *Odysseus's* hero is often brash, one who accepts cruelty, injustice, and barbarity as part of the necessary elements of life. Throughout the tragedy, he is direct, commanding, and abrupt in his singular purpose to regain his kingdom. His language, at times pejorative and misogynistic ("bitches," "hussies," "nag," "floozies"), is preserved in this translation, faithful not only to the patriarchal world of Homer's epics[14], but also to the personality of the author's Nietzschean superman. Kazantzakis's

Odysseus: A Verse Tragedy

Odysseus is not the hero who returns to Ithaca to kill his enemies and stay, but one, who stifled by the Ithaca he finds ("how can my decrepit soul / fit within a sparrow's next?"), again puts out to sea. As in Cavafy's "Ithaca"[15] what is meaningful for this Odysseus is not the arrival but the enriching experience of the voyage ("a sailor counts the entire earth his home"), who like the author's well-known character Zorba[16] wants to experience life to the fullest.

Translated into English for the first time, Kazantzakis's all-but-neglected verse tragedy *Odysseus* presents a demon-driven man, who as Kimon Friar notes, is compelled by "instinct and the promptings of the blood above the more ordered deductions of the mind"; he celebrates "the primitive and even atavistic origins of the human spirit."[17] This affirmation of life, which Odysseus proclaims even before an obliterating void, constitutes the Kazantzakian heroic character. As a complement, indeed a clarifying intensification, of the author's *The Odyssey; A Modern Sequel*, *Odysseus* brings to closure Kazantzakis's tribute to Homer and completes the evolution of the second of two major recreations of the Homeric character in Western culture — the Joycean Apollonian Ulysses (Leopold Bloom) and the Kazantzakian Dionysian Odysseus. With this translation, the English-speaking world completes its recovery of the duality of man, Odysseus Diogenes,[18] a new Odysseus for Western literature.

A Reading of Nikos Kazantzakis's *Odysseus: A Verse Tragedy*

Kostas Myrsiades

The play opens with a number of enslaved women busy filling water jugs from a near-by well and scurrying to-and-fro to no place in particular. As the sun is about to set, Melantho, the rebellious maid from Homer's epic, is the first to appear on stage, complaining of fatigue and feet made bloody from walking; like Sisyphus she has tired of her endless task of hauling water all day long. Vigla, an old woman, reprimands her and the other young maids, attributing their complaints to their annoying nightly activities, "which keeps me sleepless / all night long." The conversation shifts to blame, with the young maids accusing the older woman of jealousy at having lost her appeal to men. She retorts with threats of Odysseus's return, convinced that "you laugh now you floozies, but not one of you / will escape once he's on the island." Another maid, Leucothea, also lugging a water jug on her shoulder, puts an end to the women's bickering by announcing the imminent presence of Penelope who makes her way to Aphrodite's near-by chapel: "Our anxious queen has reached the shore / holding a basket of palms / for the sea born goddess."

Penelope has faithfully awaited her husband's return for the past twenty years and has now come to appease the goddess of love who nightly urges her to use her alluring gifts and "quickly welcome to your bed / a virile male body of your choice." Fear of Aphrodite has brought Penelope with libations to appease the goddess. Penelope is anxious to obey, "goddess, thy will be done!" Recalling Odysseus's parting words—to select a new husband once Telemachos began to show the shadow of a beard—she is now ready to listen to the goddess (and her own libido) and prays that her new union might be with Eurymachos. She then instructs Eurycleia, Odysseus's faithful old nurse, to deliver his bow to Eumaeus for stringing, for "the goddess howls, and fearful, I obey!" The nurse senses Odysseus's imminent return, however, and advises Penelope not to rush into a new marriage. For her part, the queen prefers to obey the goddess (and her own secret yearnings) and accuses the nurse of spouting nonsense. Insisting that Aphrodite is offering the queen bad advice, Eurycleia decides to say no more.

The other maids, aware of Penelope's anxiety to finish her father-in-law's shroud, interpret her housekeeper Eurynome's sighting of an eagle rapidly descending to pluck a pigeon. They declare it is a true sign from Zeus that a new bridegroom has been selected. At the very moment that the young rebel Melantho wonders who the new groom might be, the beggar, Odysseus in disguise, enters. The first word he utters is "Odysseus," responding not only to Melantho's curiosity but also ironically to his own identity, a revelation that goes unnoticed, since all the maids except for the older Eurynome who fled at his appearance. Having announced himself as Odysseus, the beggar convinces no one, including the swineherd Eumaeus, Penelope, Telemachos, and Laertes, all of whom will at different points in the drama come in direct contact with him.

Finding himself alone, the beggar bemoans his fate and calls upon Athena, who once stood by his side, to return and release him from his endless journey. Beneath his false exterior, Kazantzakis's Odysseus is, nonetheless, an unyielding and enduring colossus who depends on his own resources to rise to new challenges, determined to "conquer death again." Suddenly, Eurynome removes her maid's apron to reveal herself to the external audience as the goddess Athena. Still in disguise before Odysseus, she reminds the hero that "a mortal's heart holds the reins," the future lies in his hands. Just as Homer is clear in the first book of the *Odyssey* that although mortals blame the gods for their actions when they themselves have the power to determine their fates, so does Kazantzakis remind Odysseus that gods merely advise humans, who must accept or reject their advice. Indeed, Homer had reminded his audience that Aegisthus having rejected the gods' warning not to bed Agamemnon's wife, Clytemnestra, died for his choice at the hands of Agamemnon's son Orestes.

In a scene reminiscent of Odysseus's meeting with Nausicaa in *Odyssey*, book six, the beggar/Odysseus approaches Eurynome/Athena, first appealing to her as a goddess not to pity, but "respect / ... man's sea-drenched mind!" In the event, on the other hand, she was a mortal, he wishes her the same good fortune he offered Homer's Nausicaa: "three times blessed are your father and the lady your mother ... but blessed at the heart, even beyond these others, is that one who ... leads you as his bride home" (*Od*.6.154-160).[19]

Complimenting him on his praise, the disguised goddess asks for his name, to which he responds with a unique elaborate lie, unlike the nuanced lies Odysseus tells in Homer's *Odyssey*. Here the beggar claims to be a merchant from Phoenicia dealing in sensual paraphernalia used by women to ensnare men. The beggar admits he was a worshipper of Astarte, the Hellenized form of the ancient Near Eastern goddess Astoreth (a form of Ishtar) connected with fertility, sexuality, and war. A chief female divinity of the Phoenicians, Astarte became associated with Aphrodite, who in Kazantzakis's play represents the Dionysiac (irrational) nature of humanity while Athena represents the Apollonian (rational) nature. The beggar reveals that in his past he was a hedonist who worshipped the gifts of Aphrodite, just as, at present, Athena's temple in Ithaca remains unattended while Aphrodite's flourishes. But the hero's former pleasures are "exulted now in the ocean's depths," for he is a wretched old man, and prefers the Apollonian gifts of Athena to the Dionysian ones of Aphrodite. He asks the woman with the gentle face standing before him, who reminds him of a mortal, to identify his whereabouts. Athena/Eurynome, delighted at his cunning mind, calls him by his name and reveals her true identity.

Expressing disappointment at the absence of the goddess from his former harrowing adventures, Odysseus is nevertheless happy to see her. He again asks the name of the land in which he now finds himself and reprimands the gods for hassling a simple mortal, declaring to Athena that "I will defeat them!" Kazantzakis's Odysseus fears neither god nor man and is prepared to struggle and endure with or without anyone's help. Without further discussion, Athena assures him that he is in Ithaca, but for one who has travelled far and wide, the island seems to him too confining, "how can my decrepit soul / fit within a sparrow's nest?" To dispel any fear that the gods are once again duping him, and that he is still cast on foreign soil, Athena dissipates the mist surrounding him that he might recognize his ancestral home. Odysseus is elated, eager to dance, to lie on his belly and feel the warmth of his island's earth, to celebrate his return. Athena dampens his enthusiasm by reminding him of the struggles he has yet to overcome; she reprimands him for allowing his desires to govern his reason. Immediately, the beggar/Odysseus springs to action, "I embrace / the truth; I go forward like a god!" Both gods and men shudder at those mortals who have no fear of death, the mind that holds both life and death the same. He is ready to face whatever new trials the gods have in store for him.

Athena warns him of new troubles in his own palace and of the goddess responsible, Aphrodite, who has replaced the Apollonian goddess in his absence.

Nikos Kazantzakis

Athena's altar flame has been extinguished and she has been left whimpering with the dog Argos at the entrance. Odysseus acknowledges that of all immortals he fears Aphrodite most and considers her his great enemy. Unlike Homer's *Odyssey*, where Poseidon delays the hero's return home and nearly drowns him as he departs from Calypso for the Phaiakians, Kazantzakis's tragedy blames Aphrodite's Dionysian extremes for keeping him from home. In short, it is the body's desires (the irrational self) that prevent the hero from reaching Ithaca. Released from her influence, and having embraced the mind (Athena), Odysseus is free to tackle the "freeloaders" (the suitors) and promises to decapitate them before Athena's altar. But he hesitates to act. He asks for advice from the goddess, who offers him two options: "yes and no"; he must choose to act or not.

Having received Athena's response, beggar/Odysseus enquires about his son and father. Telemachos in adulthood no longer wants to remain in his father's shadow; as in Homer's epic, he has journeyed to Sparta to learn of his father's fate so he might free himself. Kazantzakis's Telemachos has matured much more quickly than Homer's. As for Laertes, Athena says, "he's an infant again," and his memory of Odysseus is fading. Eager for revenge, the goddess warns him to bide his time and "muzzle / like a dog your heart from barking!" Seeing Eumaeus approaching, the goddess reminds Odysseus as she exits to steel his heart, bide his time, and endure.

Beggar/Odysseus, daunted by the swineherd Eu-

Odysseus: A Verse Tragedy

maeus's advanced age, wishes to embrace him and reveal his true identity but restrains himself. Lost in blaspheming those who rebelled against the order of the palace, Eumaeus is oblivious of the stranger's presence. When he hears moaning, he thinks it's Laertes and calls out to him; instead, the beggar steps forward, presenting himself as a stranger seeking hospitality. The swineherd welcomes him and cautions patience and respect for the gods, since man's lot is one of suffering. The beggar takes exception, unwilling to blame everything on Fate. Posing as a merchant sailor, he kisses the earth and calls out, "My fatherland!" When Eumaeus asks whether he is a native of Ithaca, the beggar replies that a sailor counts the entire earth his home. The swineherd then invites him to share his dinner if he can only calm his frenzy, but the beggar would rather have him join in a dance to recall their youth. Beggar/Odysseus is here presented as one who embraces life to the fullest in spite of the fact that "this callous earth ... swallows me!" He seeks to devour everything in sight but feels inadequate and ill equipped to experience the universe without discerning between grief and joy.

The beggar asks Eumaeus to treat him as if he is receiving an old friend returning from a twenty-year journey. He shouts, "I'm back, kiss me!" At the same time that he pretends to reveal himself to Eumaeus, he conceals his identity by identifying himself as Daedalus, an Athenian scholar, who while studying in Egypt sprouted wings to escape the confines of book learning and experience unburdened life itself. Appropriating the Daedalus myth of the Cretan architect who built King Minos's maze to imprison the Minotaur and was then imprisoned himself to keep its exit a secret, the beggar seeks release to fully experience life. Claiming he saw Odysseus on one of his voyages, he continues his tale over Eumaeus's objections in being repaid for his kindness with lies.

Nevertheless, the beggar's insistence that he saw Odysseus in Calypso's arms turns into a renunciation of his former life. He blames a figuration of his alter ego for succumbing to a woman's love and betraying his country and his obligations. His alter ego responds by asking, who would abandon Olympos for the earth? In short, why give up a life of pleasure for something less. He points out that Penelope is now old. Telemachos has become his own man and forgotten his father; if he is truly Odysseus's son, he is now able to fend for himself. The beggar/Odysseus intends "to abandon my mortal self / and become immortal!" It appears, from what the beggar reveals, that Odysseus throughout his absence had been caught in a struggle between his Dionysian earth-bound self and the higher more rational Apollonian one. With his voyage concluded, he will have shed matter for spirit; he will have rejected Aphrodite's gifts and the desires of the body for those of Athena and the mind.

The beggar/Odysseus continues with his tale concerning the last time he saw Odysseus. He claims it was two months ago when he saw him heading home around Pylos's shores and addressed him, "Didn't the goddess's bed suit you any longer?" Odysseus stared

Odysseus: A Verse Tragedy

straight ahead without acknowledging him. Here, it is clear that Odysseus's long arduous journey is about to end. He is resolved upon rejecting his Dionysian self. Eumaeus is not convinced, however, even as the stranger assures him his master will return, "look there, can't you see him? / He's back!" Eumaeus, frightened and hopeful at the same time, senses a divinity in his hut and asks Linos, his young servant, to light a fire. Irritated at Eumaeus's uneasy prancing, the young servant leaves the hut, informing the two elders that it is about time for the enslaved to have their way with the master's goods and revel with the maids in Odysseus's wide bed. The beggar insists their master will return, but Linos is happy to enjoy the chaos that Odysseus's absence has created. He places a choker around the beggar/Odysseus's neck as a welcome reminder of the suitors' intentions should the master return. Bracing himself against this humiliation, beggar/Odysseus bides his time.

Once Linos leaves the room, the beggar spies another old man approaching, being jeered at by two female servants. Eumaeus identifies the elder as the master's father, Laertes. Beggar/Odysseus, struck by his aging father, "crawling in the dirt / while his flesh decays," curses gods' gifts to mortals, which must be paid with the pain of mortality. The swineherd counsels against swearing and praises the joy of youth which cannot be canceled by life's sorrows. He warns the beggar to restrain his anger against the jeering maids, who, although enslaved, now wish to pass as ladies. Seething, the beggar longs for the day when they will hang in the courtyard and again rails the gods for their injustice.

At this point, the jeering maids enter shoving Laertes ahead of them. Laertes asks for the shroud woven for him by Penelope, which the two maids are holding and they, turning to the beggar, recount Penelope's weaving trick.[20] When the beggar asks what happens now that the shroud is finished, Eumaeus says Penelope is tired of the deception, but he refuses to disclose any further household secrets to strangers. The maid Leda volunteers that Penelope finished weaving out of boredom, having to sleep without a man for such a long time. Laertes stumbles and the maids, pushing him, laugh, infuriating beggar/Odysseus who rushes to rescue him. When Laertes inquires who is attending him, the beggar replies, "Me! Father," a phrase taken by those present as an endearing reply to an older man. But the beggar cries out, "Your son is alive! Do you hear? Your son is alive!" to which Eumaeus responds with the admonition, "you can't warm a dead carcass!" Still, the beggar encourages Odysseus's return, slowly reviving Laertes, who begins to envision his son, "there he is!" and is anxious to hear more.

The scene next shifts to Telemachos's entrance, who has recently returned from seeking news of his father. The prince begins by thanking Athena for rescuing him from the suitors; in Homer's *Odyssey* they secretly planned to murder him before he came ashore but were deceived by the goddess who had him disembark before reaching Ithaca's harbor and go directly to Eumaeus's hut. In an ironic twist, Eumaeus greets him like a father welcoming a long-lost son, while his real

Odysseus: A Verse Tragedy

father, the beggar, holds back his feelings as he gazes upon his son for the first time since Telemachos was a newborn twenty years earlier. Listening to Eumaeus's advice to Telemachos, advice that he himself should be giving, he rises to blurt out, "My child!" Startled, Telemachos greets the stranger while Eumaeus interrupts to inquire about the prince's news. Instead of reporting on his mission, however, Telemachos reveals how overwhelmed he was by the wonders he experienced as a first-time traveler away from home. Stupefied by Menelaos's wealth, he relates how he had to repress his enthusiasm as he gazed at the richness about him, cautioning himself, "Telemachos, look upon / this glory and wealth with ease; / don't gape like a country bumpkin!" He is so awed by what he experienced at the Spartan court that he can't stop rambling. Eumaeus tries to interrupt him, "I'm out of breath, I tremble...." Telemachos, oblivious to everyone around him, recounts his first glimpse of Helen, "My heart went limp; she appeared a goddess." Eumaeus again interjects to curse "witless beauty," but Telemachos is unstoppable. He cannot get over Helen's beauty. For a third time Eumaeus interjects, "I'm anxious to hear about your father!" but Telemachos, undaunted, keeps singing Helen's praises, "Glory to the youth that perished for your cause." Like all young men in Kazantzakis's tragedy, he is overpowered by his Dionysian urges. He has not yet experienced the suffering, endurance, and experience that allows one to shed physical demands (Dionysian) for the higher needs of the spirit (Apollonian).

When Eumaeus finally cries out, "Oh god, my good

master is lost forever," Telemachos praises his father's deeds at Troy, which have become material for song, and prays the gods grant him the same fate. Unlike the Homeric Telemachos, Kazantzakis's character is animated and more youthful with raging hormones once in Helen's presence. He is happy to suppose his father dead in the service of such a beauty and wishes the same for himself. The disguised Odysseus is both taken aback at being considered dead and pleased that his son takes such pride in his father's efforts to retrieve Helen. Eumaeus, on the other hand, laments his master's passing and wonders who will take on the role of avenger in place of his master. Whereas Eumaeus cries for Odysseus's loss, Telemachos rejoices that praise songs rather than laments have marked his passing. He is ready to take his father's place, "to fight in Greece." Beggar/Odysseus is elated to have beside him in his golden years such a worthy son, a man of strength and honor. When the swineherd asks Telemachos if he performed last rites for his father, the prince returns to Helen, who drugged his wine with secret herbs to rouse him out from under his father's shadow to reach and even excel him. Excited by the prince's enthusiasm, the beggar encourages him to act, "pick up his [Odysseus's] spear / and head for the palace for revenge!", while keeping hope alive for his father's return, mindful of the dark blood that will be spilled to avenge the suitors' shameless disregard for hospitality. Kazantzakis's Odysseus throughout the play demands action, blaspheming the gods for mortals' lot, which ends in death. He blames humans for wallowing in debauchery and not rising above their mortality. Maintaining his disguise throughout the tragedy, beggar/Odysseus's speech and actions consistently characterize him as someone bigger than life, bursting through his beggar rags. Listening to his rantings, Eumaeus remarks, "Old man you change before my eyes; you come alive!"

While Telemachos seems ready to act, he balks as he realizes the number of suitors he must deal with by himself, a number considerably reduced from the 108 suitors and servants in Homer's *Odyssey*. In Kazantzakis's tragedy, beggar/Odysseus advises the prince how to handle their numbers: "By not counting!" Probing whether the gods will support him, Telemachos listens to the beggar articulate the play's philosophy: the gods support the victors so they can feed on their leftovers. Once man conquers Death by learning to go beyond the bounds of mortality, he can grasp that his heart is the seed of freedom. Hearing beggar/Odysseus, Telemachos imagines his father; Eumaeus fears that should the beggar stand up, his head would pierce the ceiling, since he rants and raves "like a demanding god." The swineherd is anxious to know the beggar's identity, and beggar/Odysseus both discloses it and lies about the very identity he offers. He claims not to be a phantom but a cunning survivor, a spinner of tales, a merchant, Daedalus and Odysseus himself. To maintain his deception, he requests a blanket to stretch out in the courtyard, since the wine his host offered gave him a swollen head.

Eurycleia next enters holding the great bow and

cursing the day she was born. Seeing her, Eumaeus anticipates more misfortunes to follow. Telemachos is aghast to see his father's bow in her hands. Catching sight of the prince, the old maid welcomes him home and enquires about her master. Eumaeus interjects that Odysseus "decays in the ocean's depths," but the maid is optimistic. In her mind's eye, Odysseus is already in Ithaca preparing the nets to ensnare the suitors. Discerning the beggar, she takes him as one of the many paupers who "pester my master / like crows over carrion." Although it is Eurycleia who first identifies the beggar's true identity in Homer's *Odyssey* while washing his feet, in Kazantzakis's tragedy the beggar remains incognito despite his many sarcastic hints at his identity. Telemachos interrupts Eurycleia to ask why the bow was removed from its post, but the maid is reluctant to answer until pressured. She then confesses it was Penelope's wish after Aphrodite ordered her in a dream, "Take down your husband's bow / and announce a contest to the suitors." Crediting the bow contest to Aphrodite, rather than to Penelope as Homer does, Kazantzakis lays the blame for the chaos in Ithaca on Aphrodite. Here, the goddess of love represents the libidinous desires of man and not simply love and beauty. She not only acts as the patroness of the suitors, but, as we will shortly learn, also of Penelope. In the past Odysseus himself, we are told, was an ardent worshipper of Aphrodite and all she represents. But he has now outgrown this level of human existence, and has accepted the ennobling and elevating intervention of Athena's gifts—reason, the Apollonian self—while Penelope and the suitors still remain in Aphrodite's grip.

Eurycleia has come to Eumaeus to make ready the bow for the contest, "rub it down with fat and make it pliable." At this point the beggar can no longer contain himself, "I'm going to speak if it kills me!", and he lapses into a critique of fame, and what he sees as Penelope's fidelity now turned false. He blames the immortals, who refuse to answer mortal prayers unless they receive substantial payment. Eurycleia urges Telemachos to prove he's Odysseus's son, but Eumaeus silences her, fearing for Telemachos's life. At this point, the beggar/Odysseus becomes more forceful. He urges the prince to take charge, but Telemachos chooses caution over immediate action. When the beggar encourages him to speak forthrightly, the prince decides to let Fate choose his mother's new husband, for he has lost interest, "why control my own life any longer?" Disappointed, beggar/Odysseus explains that Helen's encouraging words to Telemachos were a waste of time. But the prince lacks allies and complains that, without his father, he is helpless. The beggar advises him to rely on the bow and his own strength, and grabbing the bow, he places it in Eumaeus's hands, "to harness it / with bull-like strength lest overuse shatter it!" The beggar's zeal for action and his reliance on personal ability puts his identity into question again. The swineherd is by now convinced that the beggar is not Daedalus; before he can utter the name on the tip of his (and Eurycleia's) tongue, the beggar laughs, preventing them from blurting it out. Perhaps intended for Telemachos, the beggar identifies himself as a bard, like the one Homer's Agamemnon left behind in Mycenae to guard his faithless wife (*Od*.1.32-43).[21]

When the king returned from Troy, the bard in Kazantzakis's tragedy implored him to kill his wife Clytemnestra, "the cunning viper that lurks before you." Since Fate cannot be vanquished, however, Kazantzakis's beggar curses the indifferent Olympian gods who have little respect for mortals and "praise Injustice on their knees!" He calls Zeus a debaucher of women whom he exposes as nothing more than "a scarecrow in space." Thus, without fear, the beggar treads the earth as if it is his to harvest. The prince, intrigued, asks the beggar whether he's afraid. He responds, "Of whom?", explaining to him again the philosophy he has espoused throughout his arrival: learn to rely only on yourself; only deeds and not words count. If Telemachos can bend the bow, his father exists within him; if he cannot, his father will never arrive. When Eumaeus asks Telemachos where he is going, suddenly the prince replies "Home!" The beggar's words had "scorched [his] brain," and full of shame, he is ready to take on the suitors alone. Eumaeus tries to discourage the prince from embracing rash actions, but the beggar responds, "I despise the one who waits forever!"; one should take into account only one's strength and one's many obligations and act.

Listening to the beggar, Telemachos's anger, which he claimed to have inherited from his father, rises; he is ready for action. Eurycleia admires the prince's high-mindedness, and Eumaeus prays that he inherit his father's cunning. The two elderly servants' acco-

Odysseus: A Verse Tragedy

lades remind Telemachos of the story he heard concerning his father's spying mission to Troy, which he heard from Helen. It is the same tale Helen recites to Telemachos in Homer's epic (*Od*.4.240-264), but with a difference. Although Kazantzakis's tragedy begins with Odysseus as beggar in Ithaca and concludes when he is about to begin the slaughter of the suitors (*Od*.13-22), earlier episodes from the epic are often reworked and included in the conversations of his major characters. In Kazantzakis's version, it is Telemachos who recalls how Odysseus stole secretly into Troy as a vagabond, recognized only by Helen who kept his secret and with her help he left undetected. In his version of the tale, however, Telemachos conflates two different myths into one. In the tragedy, Odysseus's mission is not only to uncover Trojan plans, but to steal the Palladium (a wooden statue of Athena), which, an earlier prophecy had foretold, would bring victory to the Greek army. This incident was omitted from the tale recounted by Helen in the fourth book of Homer's *Odyssey*. The retrieval of the Palladium by Odysseus and Diomedes is found instead in Virgil's *Aeneid*.

The beggar now calls an end to "haughty words." He advises Telemachos to head directly to the palace and sacrifice lambs to Athena that she might aid his cause. The prince, grateful for the advice, invites the beggar to the palace the following morning to assist him, hoping that he "see in me your son restored."

Pleased, on the one hand, that his son is almost free from dependence on him, the beggar/Odysseus becomes agitated as he envisions his once faithful wife about to find a new consort with whom she will bear sons. In a last temptation reminiscent of Kazantzakis's novel, *The Last Temptation of Christ* (1955), he recalls the pleasures of his journey and for a moment wishes they would begin anew: the Sirens' "ample breasts / erect like the / circular shields of battle," the immortality offered him by Calypso, and his beast-like submission to Circe's charms. Regaining his composure, he prays that he might stand without fear on his own threshold. At that moment, Eumaeus, sleepless and thinking of the following day's contest, prays to Athena to let him be witness to the suitors' deaths, promising her a gilded yearling heifer if his wish is honored. He is still troubled by the beggar's identity, and asks for patience to do his part when the time comes. With this reminder of the identity theme, part one of the tragedy is brought to a close.

Part two of the tragedy *Odysseus* takes place on the following morning in the courtyard of the hero's palace. The emphasis shifts from a focus on the beggar and the household servants to the beggar and the suitors. Here, Kazantzakis incorporates material from Homer's *Odyssey* (books 13-22) to shape the character of the suitors and that of servants who are reintroduced from part one. Of Homer's 108 suitors, Kazantzakis uses only five, the two leaders (Antinoos and Eurymachos) and three others (Leodes, Agelaos, and Ktesippos). Of the household servants, four Homeric characters reappear (Eumaeus, Eurycleia, Eurynome, and Melantho), while all others are Kazantzakis's own creations.

Part two of *Odysseus* opens with Eurymachos, Penelope's preferred suitor, demanding that Aphrodite grant him success in the contest to reward him for favoring her over Athena. Should she "refuse to champion me," he warns, he will renounce and consign her to the "taverns and sleazy harbors" where he first encountered her. The implication is that the goddess of sensual pleasure is inferior to the goddess of wisdom, even as Eurymachos, and the other suitors, have sold their souls for physical pleasure. Antinoos responds that his fellow suitor is better off drinking and carousing with the maids, for his supplications to "the ruthless Lady" are in vain. A third suitor, Leodes calls the court bard, Phemios, who is plagued with premonitions of Odysseus's return, to sing for them.

The opening scenes of the second part of the tragedy are filled with foreboding, for as Agelaos, a fourth suitor explains, it's twenty years since Odysseus, considered dead, left Ithaca, "a great shadow falls upon the threshold." To alleviate the overwhelming gloom, Eurymachos calls for dancing girls and wine; Phemios interrupts to recount a dream in which he saw the great bow dancing like a viper on the banquet tables and an armed Athena standing at the portal. At that very moment, Vigla, the old woman serving as the suitors' sentry, enters with the greeting, "He's here!" Taking her words to mean Odysseus's presence, the suitors are stunned and prepare for the worst. Realizing the suitors have taken her words as a sign of the king's return, she replies, "I'm speaking about Telemachos!" After she is rudely dismissed, the suitors revisit their fears of a last-minute appearance by the king, although they feel certain he is dead. Phemios picks up his lyre and plays, while the dancing girls distract those present.

While the chorus entertains, the tattered beggar enters accompanied by Eumaeus; unobserved Eumaeus places the bow on a table in the center of the banquet hall. The suitors' insults and rude behavior toward the beggar and the servant follow before Melantho enters with Kazantzakis's version of Argos, Odysseus's dog. The maid claims she saw the beggar stealthily approaching the entrance. When a very animated Argos jumped up to greet him, beggar/Odysseus grabbed him by the throat and strangled him with a passion. Phemios, interprets the incident as a bad sign and tries to leave the hall, just as Telemachos appears among the columns. The scene is in keeping with Kazantzakis's theme that Odysseus will not permit anyone or anything hinder his mission, even if it means strangling Argos, his faithful companion who, for twenty years sat on a dung heap waiting to greet his master.

Telemachos is now ready to take on the suitors, and with Athena's help "to shake the foundations of my house!" Antinoos, too, is prepared to fight but is distracted by the disruptive beggar who interferes on behalf of his son. Agelaos calls on Menytes—a figure like Iros from Homer's *Odyssey* (*Od*.18.1-105)—to dispense with the beggar, but the stranger, as in Homer's epic, shatters his opponent's jaw and mortally wounds him. The suitors marvel at the beggar's physique; once he tosses off his rags, they are reminded of Odysseus but still do not make the connection. Telemachos orders Menytes's corpse removed and turning to the beggar, informs him that Athena told him in a dream to wait for his signal. In agreement, the beggar warns the prince to be patient and wait for the right moment. Phemios, noticing the two whispering, is apprehensive.

Taking notice of the beggar weeping, Antinoos wants to know why he journeyed the world's harbors. The beggar's second lie in the play portrays him as a destitute nobleman who braved the seas for the sake of his belly. He begs Antinoos to contribute graciously to his needs and relates to him an incident from his past. He once lived in rich surroundings and had an infant son whom he hoped would surpass him in archery, but his son was enslaved by pirates. His wife's whereabouts unknown, the destitute nobleman imagines her lying in some other nobleman's bed bearing him sons. Preoccupied with the contest about to begin and Penelope's fidelity on his mind since his arrival in Ithaca, the beggar/Odysseus hopes Telemachos will prove a worthy son. Antinoos, whose primary objective is to win the contest and occupy Penelope's bed, responds to the beggar's tale with a kick, causing the beggar to lose his balance and almost fall. The beggar insults the suitor by calling him stupid, and Telemachos with some authority warns the other suitors against harming the aged man. When Ktesippos and Agelaos respond by insulting the prince's absent father, calling him a cattle thief and a wily fox, the beggar soliloquizes, marveling at his ability to control his temper, "Good Lord, I might even be a god!" Telemachos rejoins the festivities extoling his father's superiority in words and deeds by recalling his role in the Wooden Horse to cause the downfall of Troy. The beggar is overwhelmed with emotion. He praises the father exalted in his old age by a son's esteem and immortalized in the memory of his offspring. Antinoos throws the beggar a bone ordering him to leave; Phemios warns of an armed Athena whom he imagines is approaching the courtyard; and the suitors continue their insults making light of their situation. The entire second part of the tragedy thus far has been slowly building to the execution of the bow contest and the revelation of Odysseus's identity. The growing tension is exacerbated by the suitors' arrogance and their obliviousness to the fragility of their position, and the foreboding of disaster, which the audience anticipates. Only Phemios, the singer of songs, crawls to embrace the beggar's knees, sensing Odysseus's presence.

Fearful of being identified, the stranger assures Phemios he is just a vagabond searching for a bite to eat. He apologizes to Antinoos for his rudeness and offers to entertain the suitors either with a dance, a bull fight, or better yet to perform Persephone's dance naked, as is the custom in his country. Persephone, wife of Hades, the god of the underworld, personifies the death that is about to visit the suitors. The beggar requests that Phemios accompany his dance with the song about the "heroes building a castle / to escape their end." The bard begins anticipating that Death will presently make his entrance to escort the suitors to Hades, as the song implies. When the singer realizes what his singing denotes for those gathered in the courtyard, he weeps; Eurymachos and Antinoos, professing their

Odysseus: A Verse Tragedy

fearlessness, encourage him to continue accompanying the naked beggar.

During the nude dance, Penelope enters, and an embarrassed beggar/Odysseus pauses to hide his nakedness. She admonishes him for not acting his age in front of youth and orders the maids to feed him. While the beggar praises the queen's beauty, she is more anxious to learn about Helen "the slut," who, despite the many deaths she caused, remains world-renowned and an object of desire. The beggar responds by elevating Penelope's fame above that of Helen's, praising her patience, her administrative skills in managing the palace, and her loyalty to a husband of whose agile mind she dreams. Thus, he not only praises the qualities he hopes she has cherished throughout his absence but also reminds her of the special qualities of the husband she lost. Penelope feigns humility, and the beggar is admonished by Agelaos to stop annoying the queen.

Eurymachos's praise of the queen's beauty and desirability opens the bow contest, which occupies the last fifth of the tragedy. He prays for the victory of the wealthiest, noblest, and wisest among them, while Antinoos interjects to include success also for the strongest. Penelope, from her observation post, is reserved and full of high praise for the "shining celestial stars," one of whom will become her new husband. She puts on a good appearance playing the faithful widow, but in reality, she's ready for male companionship as the maids earlier in the play disclosed. She calls for Aphrodite's presence, again pointing to her willingness to have a man in her life after being without one for twenty years. Phemios, who still fears a great calamity, cautions Penelope not to cross the threshold. She, feeling guiltless, is unafraid, although the bard's premonitions remind her of Odysseus's piercing eyes. Telemachos, within earshot, cries out, "Within these walls he still lives and reigns!" The queen, turning to the beggar, chastises him for swaggering like a savage and not showing greater respect for his surroundings. In response, the beggar/Odysseus imagines the earth churning like an angry sea on which Death approaches on a ship with red sails, an indication he is anxious to reveal himself and strike. His poisonous words fly like arrows from his mouth, anticipating the slaughter about to begin. Penelope reminds the beggar that she found him more genial earlier. The stranger confesses that as a warrior, he was once forgiving and would release his captives imagining they too had a faithful Penelope waiting for them. Now he has concluded that faithfulness should be flexible to the needs of passion. Recommending that Penelope make known her choice of suitor to Aphrodite, he wishes he was young enough to try his hand at the bow himself. Flattered, Penelope asks him to make room for younger men and not interfere, "We're all slaves to Fate." It seems Penelope has consigned her own urges to Fate.

Eumaeus announces that the twelve ax heads are ready and entreats Penelope to begin the contest. But before she makes the bow available, she asks for Aphrodite's blessing, again exposing her true sensibilities. In a long speech in which she tries to both conceal and justify her eagerness for a male companion, she first

Odysseus: A Verse Tragedy

asks Aphrodite to guide the hand of blind Fate. She is reminded of Odysseus's last words to her before leaving Ithaca. She was to remain faithful and care for her home and in-laws until her son showed signs of manhood. If by then Odysseus had not returned from Troy, he would have perished, and she would be free to remarry. Resolved to follow his advice and pine for him "veiled in my widow's isolation," Penelope swears she never looked at another man nor desired anyone whose qualities were less than those of Odysseus. But now "the gods command and I obey." Having fully explained away any wrongdoing, she appeals to Aphrodite "to select for me a handsome lad" to share her bed. As much as Penelope wants to be praised as a faithful, grieving widow, she also desires a new husband, preferably Eurymachos.

A chorus of female dancers intervenes to sing of Victory and of the handsome youth who will bend the bow. Beggar/Odysseus, watching and listening closely, tries to remain calm. Telemachos whispers that it's time for the beggar to give the signal for the slaughter. The beggar retorts, "It's not time yet"; God will beckon when the time is right to drag the suitors to the nets already set for them. Telemachos calls for the contest to begin, lauding his mother as a worthy prize. Phemios once more senses "the oppressive light / of death" pervading the megaron, as Leodes, the first to try the bow, fails. Antinoos announces that only he or Eurymachos have a chance for victory, and the beggar, aware of Athena's presence, prays for a sign to begin the slaughter. His answer comes through the voices of three mill women who, hearing Athena's thunderclap, beseech the goddess to grind the suitors' heads. Here Kazantzakis triples Homer's single mill woman, who hears Zeus's response to Odysseus's prayer (*Od*.20.103-119). Further, he substitutes Athena for Zeus, emphasizing the mind (Athena) over matter (Aphrodite). Entering the scene, Eurycleia interprets the thunderclap as the hooves of Odysseus's mount conveying him home after his long absence. For Odysseus, the thunder emanates from deep within the earth's bowels, a signal from his ancestors; for Telemachos, it is a sign of his ability, "I no longer set limits to my strength." The prince, no longer able to contain himself shouts, "I'm no longer satisfied bending to an old man's whims!" At this moment, when the son is no longer dependent on the father, the beggar/Odysseus cries out, "Son!" In Kazantzakis's tragedy, the recognition between father and son occurs here, just before the slaughter, rather than, as Homer has it, at Eumaeus's hut when Telemachos returns from his journey (*Od*.16.176-212). The beggar identifies himself to his son only when the son has freed himself from his father's dependence. Phemios, now turned into a reliable prophet, envisions the suitors' blood saturating the hall. Agelaos, under the influence of undiluted wine, no longer fears Odysseus's presence; Eurymachos orders the singer to leave the hall. As Phemios prepares to flee, Telemachos tries to stop him, but the beggar orders the prince to allow the singer to leave before the doors are barred. The suitors, oblivious to the doom about to befall them, continue their efforts to bend the bow. Eumaeus moves towards

Odysseus: A Verse Tragedy

the outer door where the beggar is standing and asks why he is staring; in answer beggar/Odysseus reveals an identifying scar he has had since childhood. Restraining an emotional Eumaeus from kissing his feet, the beggar entreats him to close the lower and upper floors and to remove all weapons from the walls. Penelope, glancing fearfully at the beggar's penetrating eyes admonishes the suitors' bickering over the bow and reminds them how easy a task it was for her husband. Eurymachos, hoping for victory, prays to Aphrodite to select the best among them in excellence, reason, and by birth, and Penelope hopes he will succeed. Failing at the bow, Eurymachos calls out Penelope's name, but she is no longer interested, "If you can't bend it, give it / to someone who can!" Eurymachos, humiliated to be seen as a lesser man than Odysseus, hands the bow to Antinoos. The queen, expressing little discontent at losing her favorite suitor asks who has yet to take his turn. It seems Penelope is willing to settle for anyone whose strength can match that of her absent husband.

At that moment, Laertes enters, believing that Penelope has sent for him. He explains how a blue-eyed maiden led him to the palace. Eumaeus marvels at the elder's alertness, and the beggar discerns Athena's hand in his father's presence. Penelope begins to tremble, sensing the presence of "a god ... passing / silently like an eagle in flight." Antinoos is distraught, Leodes comments that the air grows dark, Ktesippos questions the swineherd's purpose in hiding the suitors' weapons, and Telemachos asks for wine to fill the suitors' glasses. The suitors' leader, still confident of victory, is willing to allow even "the lowest of the low" to join the festivities and invites the beggar to lift his cup to toast Aphrodite. Instead of honoring Aphrodite, however, the beggar offers a libation to Athena. Suddenly, a great flame flares up from the goddess's neglected altar. Antinoos scrambles to quench it, but Telemachos, recognizing the goddess's presence, orders that no one extinguish the flame. Penelope, too, sensing she is caught in a net, detects a controlling force. Laertes raises his ancestral cup to offer a greeting, and welcomes the goddess to his polluted home, pouring three drops of wine on the earth for the grandfather, the son, and grandson. Telemachos urges Antinoos to take his turn at the bow. The suitor anxious to bed Penelope takes hold of the bow objecting to the bolted doors and the prince in arms.

At this point, Telemachos (not Odysseus as in Homer's *Odyssey*) orders the hall cleared. He asks his mother to visit Athena's altar and rekindle its fading ambers. He then orders the suitors to remain where they are, and the women to retire to the upper floor observing silence at whatever happens below. Turning to his grandfather, he seeks a blessing for himself and for his absent father. The prince has at last reached maturity and is free of his father's dominance. Beggar/Odysseus intercedes to demand the queen's presence for the remaining contestants. Antinoos, unable to bend the bow, drops it. Telemachos has Eumaeus place it in the beggar's hands, who easily strings it and shoots an arrow through the twelve ax heads. Throwing off his

Odysseus: A Verse Tragedy

rags, he signals to Telemachos and Eumaeus standing on either side of him; Laertes and Penelope in unison gasp, "Odysseus!" Odysseus, triumphant, delivers the tragedy's final lines, reminding the suitors of the bolted doors and informing them that the wedding is ready to get under way. He asks Penelope to hide in a corner lest an arrow injure her. Identifying himself to those present, and with bow in hand, he is ready to have "death [bring] / peace like a thunderbolt in the hand of justice."

Kazantzakis's *Odysseus* ends with the slaughter about to take place. What follows next will not be revealed until a decade later in Kazantzakis's verse epic, *The Odyssey; A Modern Sequel*, "And when in his wide courtyards Odysseus had cut down / the insolent youth, he hung on high his sated bow ..." (Kazantzakis, *Odyssey* I: 1-2).

SOURCES CONSULTED

Friar, Kimon. 1979. *The Spiritual Odyssey of Nikos Kazantzakis*. Minneapolis: North Central Publishing Co.

Hauptmann, Gerhart. 1917. *The Dramatic Works of Gerhart Hauptmann; Miscellaneous Dramas: Commemoration Masque, The Bow of Odysseus, Elga, Fragments: Hellos, Pastoral*. Vol. 7. Ed. Ludwig Lewisohn. New York: B.W. Huebsch.

Homer. *The Odyssey of Homer*. 2007. Tr. Richmond Lattimore. New York: HarperPerennial.

Kazantzakis, Nikos. 1953. *Zorba the Greek*. Tr. Carl Wildman. New York: Simon and Schuster.

Nikos Kazantzakis

―――. 1955. *Theatro. Tragodies me archaia themata. Prometheas, Kouros, Odysseas, Melissa.* Athens: Difros.

―――. 1957. *Epistoles ste Galateia.* Athens: Difros.

―――. 1958. *The Odyssey; A Modern Sequel.* Tr. Kimon Friar. New York: Simon and Schuster.

―――. 1976. "Drama and Contemporary Man." Tr. Peter Bien. *The Literary Review* 19.2: 115-21.

Myrsiades, Kostas. 2019. *Reading Homer's Odyssey.* Lewisburg, PA: Bucknell University Press.

Prevelakis, Pandelis. 1961. *Nikos Kazantzakis & His Odyssey; A Study of the Poet and the Poem.* Tr. Philip Sherrard. New York: Simon and Schuster.

―――. 1965. *Tetrakosia Grammata tou Kazantzakis ston Prevelaki.* Athens: n.p.

Raizis, Byron M. 1971-72. "Kazantzakis's Ur-Odysseus, Homer, and Gerhart Hauptmann." *Journal of Modern Literature* 2.2.: 199-214.

Stanford, W.B. 1963. *The Ulysses Theme.* Oxford: Basil Blackwell.

Vrettakos, N. 1980. *Nikos Kazantzakis: His Struggle and his Work.* Athens: Biblioathinaiki Publishing.

Odysseus: A Verse Tragedy

NOTES

[1] Kazantzakis is the author of thirteen novels, eighteen dramatic works (of which seven were written in verse), three philosophical studies (on Nietzsche, Bergson, and himself), a series of travel books (Greece, Spain, England, China, Japan, Israel, Russia), two books of poetry (one, *Terza Rima*, is on his influences, which include Dante, Shakespeare, St. Teresa, Moses, Mohammed, El Greco, Lenin, Don Quixote, and Ghenghis Khan), and his masterpiece, *The Odyssey*. He also wrote hundreds of articles for newspapers and encyclopedias, dozens of texts for Greek public schools, numerous translations into modern Greek (Homer's *Iliad* and *Odyssey*, Dante's *Divine Comedy*, Goethe's *Faust, Part I*, Nietzsche's *The Birth of Tragedy*, Bergson's *On Laughter*, Darwin's *The Origin of Species*), and dozens of other works.

[2] Dante, *Inferno*, Canto 26.
[3] Kazantzakis 1958, XVI.
[4] Stanford 1963, 235.
[5] Kazantzakis 1976.
[6] Kazantzakis 1976.
[7] Kazantzakis 1957.
[8] Prevelakis 1961, Part I, The Poet.
[9] Prevelakis 1965, 74, 85, 92, 94, 96, 98.
[10] Along with French translations of *Melissa*, *Julian*, and *Prometheus I*.
[11] Kazantzakis 1957, 51, 67, 88, 158.
[12] Prevelakis 1965, 180, 314, 586, 609.
[13] Hauptmann 1917.
[14] In Homer's *Iliad* a woman is worth four oxen while a tripod is worth twelve. See *Iliad* 23.700-739.
[15] C. P. Cavafy. *The Canon*. Tr. Stratis Haviaras. Harvard University Press, 2007, 90-93.

[16] Kazantzakis, *Zorba the Greek*, 1953.
[17] Kimon Friar in Pandelis Prevelakis, *Nikos Kazantzakis & His Odyssey*, 8-9.
[18] Doubly born.
[19] Homer 2007.
[20] In Homer's *Odyssey*, Penelope postponed selecting a suitor to replace her absent husband until she finished a shroud for her father-in-law Laertes. However, by unweaving at night what she had completed during the day, she was able to keep the suitors at bay for three years until one of her maids revealed her secret to them.
[21] Homer 2007.

ODYSSEUS: A VERSE TRAGEDY

Cast Of Characters

Odysseus, *king of Ithaca, who appears as a beggar throughout the play.*
Telemachos, *his son.*
Penelope, *his wife.*
Laertes, *his father.*
Athena, *goddess of reason, the mind (in opposition to the goddess Aphrodite, who represents passion).*
Eumaeus, *the noble swineherd in charge of Odysseus's pig farm.*
Linos, *Eumaeus's young male servant.*
Eurycleia, *Odysseus's old nurse.*
Eurynome, *Penelope's housekeeper and nurse.*
Melantho, *Penelope's young treacherous maid.*
Young female household servants
Chloe
Gorgo
Erifile
Leucothea

Nikos Kazantzakis

Leda
Phaedra
Vigla, *an old local woman, the suitors' sentry.*
Antinoos, *the main suitor for Penelope's hand.*
Eurymachos, *the second and favorite of Penelope's two leading suitors.*
Penelope's suitors
Leodes
Agelaos
Ktesippos
Menytes, *an Iros-like vagabond (Od.18.1-107) who fights beggar/Odysseus.*
Phemios, *a bard in Odysseus's palace.*
Chorus
Female Dancers, *young girl dancers.*
Household servants who grind wheat and barley flour
First Mill Woman
Second Mill Woman
Third Mill Woman

Part I

(*The Ithacan shore. Adjoining the sea is Aphrodite's chapel; inside the chapel a gold carved wooden image of the goddess whose two hands prop up her breasts. Outside the chapel, a circular stone rimmed well; female servants shuffle about carrying water. Set deep to the left is Eumaeus's hut, and behind it a circular fenced pen. The sun is about to set.*)

MELANTHO

Sun! you do take your time setting!
My feet are bleeding from walking on these stones.
I'm dead tired
bent over the well all day long
hauling water.

VIGLA

    Is the water jug too much for you, Melantho?
What do you expect cavorting all night long
in Eurymachos's arms.

Nikos Kazantzakis

CHLOE

    Oh, saintly night,
which subdues both gods and men,
come release us from this day's tediousness.

VIGLA

    Floozies! what's your hurry?
You annoy the entire seashore with your moaning,
which keeps me sleepless
all night long.

GORGO

    Just because your wilted body
and your once firm but now sagging breasts
can't find a man to harvest your dried-up bosom.
You enjoyed your youth
lying atop goat-footed Pan's
wooly, frizzy-haired belly,
as the caves about reverberated
with your wild erotic screams.
Now, we're the ones ripe for picking.
It's our turn to frolic
with men.

MELANTHO

    Like bronze cauldrons boiling
with passion, the gluttonous suitors

Odysseus: A Verse Tragedy

gather around the widow's exalted bed,
but she slyly avoids their advances
keeping them at bay,
while every night their passion
erupts on us, the slave women,
and fills the palace with bastard
girls and boys.

ERIFILE

    If only Odysseus turned up unexpectedly
like a lion in this sun-drenched street
wearing his cone-shaped skullcap
and grasping his man-slaughtering spear,
avoiding the prying eyes around him.
God, what an awesome sight!

CHLOE

I too would welcome such a sight.

VIGLA

To place a noose around your necks, you hussies.
Beware, he's coming!

GORGO

I'm tired of waiting like our mistress;
let him come at last and whatever must will happen.

Nikos Kazantzakis

ERIFILE

Whenever my unfortunate mother dreams of him,
she jumps out of bed petrified
as if a viper bit her in her sleep.
And I, stifling my fear, caress
and soothe her convulsing body.
"Mother," I cry, "he's dead, don't tremble!"
But she in horror shakes her white head,
and silently eavesdrops
on the thunderous sea and cries.

GORGO

But tell me, you old nag, doesn't a mortal frame
also enclose his murky soul?
Is he a devil or a bellowing god
feeding on men at sea?
Shame on those insolent youth
who sent you sentry to spy
when his rotten raging prow
will adorn our azure sea;
then they can flee like leaves in the wind.
What a disgrace for youth to fear such things.

CHLOE

Listen you, goggle-eyed old woman,
has a cat got your tongue? You're shaking.

Odysseus: A Verse Tragedy

VIGLA

Heaven, protect me; deliver me
from these blockheads who jeer at me.
But my cries fall on deaf ears.
You laugh now you floozies, but not one of you
will escape once he's on the island.
I know the cunning rogue he is;
he's patient, evasive, and suddenly
at the right moment
when you least expect it, he's on top of you!
Then "let earth part and swallow me,"
and you're free from care.
Merciless will be the slaughter on your heads.
If you run away,
he'll still catch you
and lynch one after another in the courtyard;
your delicate little hands
won't even have time to touch his knees in supplication.

MELANTHO

I pray to you mistress Aphrodite
of the unbridled sea. Deny his homecoming.
Grasp both father and son by their feet
and smash their heads upon the rocks!

LEUCOTHEA

(Appears carrying a water jug on her shoulder.)

Nikos Kazantzakis

Sisters keep quiet, don't shout!
She's making her way through the olive grove.
Our anxious queen has reached the shore
holding a basket of palms
for the sea-born goddess.

MELANTHO

She's bringing white pigeons
for your altar again, Ladylove,
lest you complain. But you, Lady,
enraged, pound on her bedposts,
hungry for a man to satisfy your passion.

CHLOE

How delicately she treads the earth
and strolls so gracefully.

GORGO

In the rear her old granny shakes
her all-white head,
as new calamities again absorb her.

ERIFILE

How her spotless sea-drenched body dazzles.
As if the yearning of so many men rekindle it,
surrounding her like deer
dying of thirst before a spring.

Odysseus: A Verse Tragedy

MELANTHO

How does she fend off the best
from her bed at night?

GORGO

She controls her longing wisely
dallying with love coyly,
always keeping her honor lofty.

VIGLA

Fill your water jugs and withdraw
from the sacred well dutifully and silently.
Penelope raises her hands
and approaches.

PENELOPE

    Mistress, of the beguiling smile,
with hands clasped about your ample holy bosom,
you appeared in my dreams last night,
and frightened me, my Lady.
Your sacred eyebrows moved waveringly,
tossing my bed sheets aside,
and your cry made my bed quiver,
"You sleep alone
and scorn the alluring gifts of Aphrodite
that soothe even the beasts of burden? Rise;
you're destined to quickly welcome to your bed

a virile male body of your choice
and together take pleasure in my all-consuming lust
that veils the earth,
and like newlyweds seek my blessing."
"Lady"—I screamed—"I fear your anger
and at night from deep within me
secret voices emerge to cloud my reason,
which till now like a guiding light
channeled my words and actions.
I sense your hands on me,
and your command takes hold
and controls my mind and being.
What freedom can I enjoy in gods' fathomless design
but to minister to you?"
You draw near with your scheming smile,
sweetly assail my body and declare,
"Through my voice Fate dictates
that you remove Odysseus's heavy bow,
that indomitable weapon inactive upon the column,
and the suitor whose strength
instantly bends
that formidable weapon
and casts an arrow through twelve ax heads,
willing or not, you will be his wife."
It is with such harsh rapport, Omnipotence,
that you plague my sleep with smiles.
How can a mortal
fight immortals? You lead me
before your altar a willing slave, and I proffer
twin pigeons to appease you.
But if these white feathers are not enough,

Odysseus: A Verse Tragedy

and you seek a man to delight my womanly frame,
then goddess, thy will be done!
I grasp your knees; bow before you
to whisper a secret in your ear:
"Aphrodite, enrapturing sister
of death and unwearied weaver of life,
heed my secret yearning.
Since my lifetime partner is fated
to drown in the azure waves,
and black Fate forces me to welcome
a new husband to my untainted bed"
—at your feet I bow my Lady—
"grant your blessings on Eurymachos!"

And you, good Eurycleia when evening comes
remove the wall-mounted bow
from the colossal column and deliver it
this very evening to the old swineherd
to newly string and with vigilant patience
rub it down with oil.
The goddess howls, and fearful, I obey!

EURYCLEIA

My child, a thousand ills befall
the mortal soul when it ages,
but the gods instinctively mollify the years,
and when the mind begins to falter,
they endow us with a mantic vision
to augur the future and the past.
And now on death's doorstep,

Nikos Kazantzakis

by divine right I can see clearly,
and with ease I prophesy before I die.
Queen, in my heart I see
his foam-drenched prow
swiftly cleave the sea and come within sight.
He'll come, he'll come, don't be hasty, my child.
Hour by hour, I count the time —
the twenty years have not yet passed;
a single day, the most momentous still remains.
Gods' promised pledge cannot be cracked,
for gods are immortal,
and patience is a stately gift.

PENELOPE

The twenty years are gone good woman,
and he sojourns only in our minds.
My son, flailed by waves, is at risk
in search of his world-renowned father.
I sense it in my heart, direct from immortal
godly mouths, which never lie:
Odysseus is dead!

EURYCLEIA

He only died in your heart, my lady.

PENELOPE

Your bountiful love has addled your mind,
and you babble nonsense.

Odysseus: A Verse Tragedy

EURYCLEIA

          My eyes
pierce the darkness like a bat
and expose the mysteries of the palace.
Upon the altar of your undiscerning
and ungirded Lady, I openly allege:
every night this goddess offers you bad advice,
but I hold my tongue; a slave can say no more.

PENELOPE

I too keep silent; only before the gods
my words remain sincere.

(*They exit.*)

ERIFILE

Good news! Before long the sacrificial nuptial lambs
will be bleating in our courtyard.

MELANTHO

That's why the widow spends so many nights
finishing her father-in-law's shroud.
Her loom is in overdrive,
and the maids hastily stitch the fringes.

CHLOE

Quickly let's head for the palace.

Nikos Kazantzakis

I sense fear
in the evening air.

EURYNOME

(*Enters breathless*)

We're lost!

VIGLA

    Did he come?

EURYNOME

        Oh my, what a disaster!

ALL TOGETHER

Blessed Aphrodite, deliver us!

EURYNOME

On the left as I approached the palace,
I saw a great eagle spread
colossal beating wings, shrieking
and dropping like death upon our courtyard.
Alarmed the pigeons soared
with sorrowful cries—
their shadows darkening the sky.

Odysseus: A Verse Tragedy

MELANTHO

Receive warmly this confirming sign
and raise your hands in gratitude.
Inform me Zeus, who is the lucky one,
to whom you send your radiant raptor from on high,
the swift messenger of matrimony?
Kudos to you, predestined groom,
whose soft caresses
will make Penelope's withered frame flower.
Like pigeons, the suitors take flight.
Who is the groom the eagle plucked?

ODYSSEUS

                    Odysseus!
Hey bitches! Where am I? Wait!

(*The maids flee tightlipped; only Eurynome remains behind.*)

You try my patience, you fiends
and whatever logical thoughts remain, I misplace.
You confound my mind with illusions
and nurture my heart's hunger
with flights of fancy.
Once again, the Sirens spring before me on my journey,
poised erect, chanting in the wind,
and their voracious voices
balance my soul between a yes and no.
Rise Odysseus, bend your agile mind
like a bow and rend the mist.

Nikos Kazantzakis

Do I reason like a mortal? In my breast
I embrace a god as I cast about.
Yet I battle the Stygian waves,
and, clinging to the waterlogged tiller,
I conquer death again. Lightning bolts
blind me, and my godlike mind blurs.
"Athena, Athena" —I shout—"release me!
Prevent the gods, my Lady
from using me as fodder for carrion crows.
Burst from my head fully armed.
Recall the many years we strove together,
you bunkered down on my brow
as I lay in the sun.
Descend upon the earth
and tend my haughty heart lest it burst."

(*Eurynome removes her maid's apron and appears as Athena.*)

EURYNOME/ATHENA

Old-timer, why are you shouting?
Why yank your hair like an offended widow?
On your feet! Haven't you learned
after so many years to govern terror?
And yet you're not timid;
you stand on your own two feet
with soul and body well suited to each other.
Brace yourself! It's time to cast your willpower
like a spear on Fate's scale,
and it will tip your way,
since a mortal's heart holds the reins.

Odysseus: A Verse Tragedy

ODYSSEUS

Your words land on my heart
like aged wine, which rouses
manhood and steadies wobbly knees.
In looks and stature you appear a goddess,
and I kneel to kiss your immortal feet.
Behold how the sea has battered me
like a pebble, and heaved me about
on the surface of massive waves.
I seek not pity but respect
for man's sea-drenched mind.
Lay hands on me and set a castaway
free from both earth and sea.
However, if you're the offspring of mortals
blessed is your father and mother
and thrice blessed the man
who will share your nuptial bed.

ATHENA

Your tongue rebounds stranger, as it weaves
its praise and manipulates the shuttle,
embroidering timely ornaments on its cloth.
But first reveal your lawful name
and the council that adjudged you to the waves?

ODYSSEUS

I'm a merchant from Phoenicia
called Much-enduring.

Nikos Kazantzakis

In my swift ship I sailed
the azure seas of Greece
dealing in fancy fragrances,
multi-breasted goddesses, coarse demons
and translucent magnets, and even spiders.
On crouching slave women such trinkets
came across as a sky full of stars,
which even Athena would proclaim:
"Whose hands dare vie my immortal ones?"
Wondrous relics, I sold to women,
holy poisonous herbs
that conferred double youth to those late in life
and cryptic pleasures to dames and old maids
to beguile passers-by while seated on their stoops.
Also, mysterious trifles, secret makeup,
curly-haired phalluses and magic mirrors.
I sold everything a woman needs, My Lady,
to ensnare her man.
And every evening mother Astarte's blessings
were upon us night and day—
that earthen form replete
with weighty breasts that resuscitate life.
I worshipped her, prostrate on the seashore
hoping to bring profit to my trade.
Oh, young maidens, to repose on an evening
upon the warm Phoenician sands
at Astarte's vermilion feet
during our erotic drunken festivals.
One could sweetly coo sighs like a turtledove
and embraced, shout: "Never again
will I return to Greece."

Odysseus: A Verse Tragedy

ATHENA

What sweetness trickles from your lips.
Like a honeybee sensing an exquisite flower,
my soul remains sleepless at your words.

ODYSSEUS

Wretched, I reconstruct my former fortunes,
forgetting how my journey went,
exulted now in the ocean's depths.
And you, Poseidon, frightful master
of the seas, who disrespects man's
grief and efforts,
the day will come to give account.

Fair lady, in your gentle face
I glimpse mortality and compassion,
pity an old man and make known to me
on whose land again the gods have set me.
Why are you silent? Tell me the whole truth
and don't be troubled. My heart endured
far and wide; to hear the truth,
it is now capable and willing.

ATHENA

Cunning, long-suffering Odysseus,
who suckled falsehoods at the breast.
Your mind like a deep-water fisherman's
strives to cast far its tightly woven nets.

Nikos Kazantzakis

Your agile mind
is like a honeycomb that slowly drips its honey.
For your devotion, I nurtured you
and from Olympos's highest peak
toiled to deify your hands and mind.
Now necessity dispatches me and here I am,
like an amazon by your side.

ODYSSEUS

Athena!

ATHENA

   Don't be frightened!

ODYSSEUS

       You arrive now
when I find myself on terra firma
and no longer fear the gaping mouth of Ocean.
But where was your love, Athena,
when you sauntered with the gods,
as I struggled on the rotten raft and in the cave?
Now you stand beside me
to easily share my current feats.
Yet I love you, for only you
reveal to me Olympos's secrets.
Come near me loyal companion
of mortals and whisper the name
of the land the gods have cast me.

Odysseus: A Verse Tragedy

Shame on the immortals
to hassle a fleeting mortal.
And yet, I will defeat them!

ATHENA

You stand on native soil
and bend like a slender bow,
oblivious.

ODYSSEUS

    My mind takes flight!
This barren island, this narrow wasteland
devoid of water and light, utterly beguiles
and restrains me; how can my decrepit soul
fit within a sparrow's nest?
Where is our towering mountain,
the thickset trees, and our round fathomless lakes?
How self-effacing and bare it all seems.
You can't deceive me; again, I'm cast
on foreign shores, and dispatched Nereids
fool me. Yet, I'm unwilling
to be indebted to you.

ATHENA

Don't beat your head against the rocks,
but open wide your eyes with gratitude.
Look, I dissipate the mist:
there lies your native mountain;

its defiant trees murmuring on its slopes.
There the olive groves, the vineyards, and the pines.
Before you spread out, the windless lake.
There the Nymphs' cave with its single olive tree;
nearby old Eumaeus's hut,
and the divine arresting view of Ithaca.

ODYSSEUS

Oh, land of my fathers,
ancestral seashore, forests, and mountains.
I feel entrenched again in my country.
I accrue new energy and sprout
new roots like an enduring oak.
Oh, Ithaca, Telemachos, wife,
and sacred smoke rising above the roof
of my paternal home; holy burial grounds
on the edge of open sea, I greet you all!

ATHENA

Brace yourself and point your prow
toward new mortal struggles.

ODYSSEUS

Hush and move aside so I can dance,
and like a dog lay upon the earth
to cool the bottom of my belly.
If only my small island
were an infant's fragile form
to cradle within my palms.

Odysseus: A Verse Tragedy

ATHENA

Shame! To behave like an adolescent,
since by now you comprehend the human soul,
and must weigh all things
within your nimble mind.
A shame to allow the heart to judge
in times of danger.

ODYSSEUS

      Athena, honor the whole truth,
and I go forward like a god.

ATHENA

I salute you, for never to falsehood
nor to risk did you ever cry: "Enough!"

ODYSSEUS

Heroic deeds I find overtly selfish;
gods and men shudder at the mind
that wisely looks both ways
and holds life and death the same.
Speak unflinchingly goddess of new trials
unleashed to be numbered among my own.

ATHENA

Take note that troublemakers celebrate your life,

merrymaking to the melody of the lyre,
which resonates in your halls throughout the day.

ODYSSEUS

And which of the gods dares allow it?

ATHENA

Aphrodite.

ODYSSEUS

      Once again, she reaches out
her soft hands to drown me.
Be aware that of all great immortals,
I fear none as much.

ATHENA

      Rejoicing, the maids
ravaged my altar and extinguished
its flame from your courtyard.
And like a whipped dog in heat,
I whimper with faithful Argos at the entrance,
but on her altar a reeking smell ascends
slowly to nourish her immoral body.

ODYSSEUS

Don't fret, goddess, for I mean to bury
all these freeloaders and, like sacrificial bulls,

decapitate them before your altar,
and snuff out their bawdy songs
to silence their harsh-sounding lyre.
Yet a snake still coils around my soul.
Reply, Athena! Flash before my eyes
what I want to ask but cannot say.

ATHENA

Two options are attainable.
Yes and no!

ODYSSEUS

    Your words are few but to the point goddess:
yes or no.
And my son?

ATHENA

    He was waiting for his father
and regardful of his earliest memory of you
was working to imitate you; but now …

ODYSSEUS

                      Now?

ATHENA

He's come of age
and no longer wants to remain in his father's shadow.

Nikos Kazantzakis

He's off to Sparta to ascertain your death
and finally shed your royal carcass
from his shoulders so he can breathe ...
if you're dead, rest in peace.

ODYSSEUS

I'm better off dead ...
and my old man?

ATHENA

    He's an infant again.

ODYSSEUS

        Does he remember me?

ATHENA

His mind withers;
everything clouds over; he's burned-out,
and you're fading from his mind.

ODYSSEUS

Immortals, I extoll you,
although once again you pelt my white head
with torments. My agile mind
like an octopus with endless tentacles
and seven lives roams the salty brine.

Odysseus: A Verse Tragedy

When one is lost, a colossal
other takes its place, replete with mouth and hungers.

ATHENA

Don't be in a hurry; hold tight the reins
and control your rage and ardor.
And when you catch sight of home,
muzzle like a dog your heart from barking!

ODYSSEUS

You need not counsel me, I understand very well
to keep my thoughts to myself.

ATHENA

It's time for me to leave; I see your faithful
swineherd panting by the rocks.
Look at him struggling, remember him?
Don't tremble. Crying my esteemed Odysseus?
How fast you mislay your heroic stature.
It's time to show endurance.
And when you happen upon those you cherish,
how will you act? Rise up, steel yourself
and drown your every futile yearning.
Knock dauntlessly
on your palace door,
even though your lion heart crumbles;
the time for your assault will come, embrace it.

(*Athena exits. Eumaeus enters.*)

Nikos Kazantzakis

ODYSSEUS

How you aged faithful Eumaeus.
Your knees shake from age,
and your hair is entirely white.
If only I could embrace you in my arms
and with joy and sadness
reveal my royal name to lighten my burden.

EUMAEUS

Damn the lot! Zeus above,
gentle and infallible,
with steady hands you weigh what is just.
May your thunder and double lightning bolts
blast open this solid earth
and swallow up the anarchists,
lest anyone again trample on divine justice.
They leap and frolic like fish
in the early morning dew,
and suddenly the fisherman's net ensnares them.
Yes, Zeus, you keep a night-long vigil
and handily work the trawl-line.

Who is it? I hear tears of mourning;
it's probably Laertes. Don't rush old timer
to enter the Field of Asphodel,
although it's time to begin your homeward journey.
Stop weeping. Tonight, I'll bring a gift,
your daughter-in-law's latest shroud,
double folded and closely woven,
to royally wrap your bony form three times over

Odysseus: A Verse Tragedy

lest you be embarrassed before Hades.
Where are you? The blind lead the blind.
My eyes cloud over and ache,
and my ears hum like seashells.
Laertes, dear companion, show yourself!

ODYSSEUS

May the gods grant you sight
to look upon whatever your heart desires, old timer.
I'm a stranger who honors your dwelling's hearth.

EUMAEUS

My god, what voice robs me of my thoughts
and compels me to abandon hope?
Speak to me, old man, don't cringe!
It seems your woes have bent your mind.
Patience! Upon this earth we luck upon sorrows,
and it's a sin to overlook them.

ODYSSEUS

You unburden your heart in haste
and blame it all on Fate; I don't agree!

EUMAEUS

You shake your head arrogantly
and show little respect
to the divinities to whom we must bow.

Nikos Kazantzakis

ODYSSEUS

Don't scold me. If you only knew the burdens
the immortals heaped on me.
Is it for them we struggle?
Let me hold tight your honest hand;
gripping it, I might forget my problems.

EUMAEUS

I grieve the way you look, and the way you hold me.

ODYSSEUS

I supplicate your feeble body
for salvation, father,
and I embrace your wobbly knees
and hands calloused by hard labor.
Do not abandon a merchant sailor
hardened by life. I fall upon this rock
and kiss it with tears and laughter ...
Fatherland! My fatherland!

EUMAEUS

          Who are you?
Are you perhaps a native of Ithaca?

ODYSSEUS

Which Ithaca? Be aware, old timer,

Odysseus: A Verse Tragedy

a sailor counts the entire earth his home.

EUMAEUS

Listen, don't lash out;
control your anger;
accept my invitation to sup with me.
Sweet wine and wheaten bread
can subdue a wild heart
and soothe a savage breast.

ODYSSEUS

I don't want to calm down.
Stand up! Let's dance
and recall our stolen youth.

EUMAEUS

           Good God, where does the human
heart of clay get the energy
to sing in the snares of death!

ODYSSEUS

I can't get enough of kissing
this callous earth that swallows me.

EUMAEUS

My mind goes numb and boils over.

Nikos Kazantzakis

ODYSSEUS

Nature can no longer contain me,
and I detest my unworthy soul,
unable to embrace even this little island.

EUMAEUS

You must have suffered many ills battling waves,
and now long to embrace the earth,
hoping to find her a friend
to mortals.

ODYSSEUS

    My mind is heavy;
my eyes, aghast, soak up everything.
I'm an uncontrollable flood
spilling eight seas over flat ground,
drowning gods, animals, and mortals.

EUMAEUS

Come in. Stop fighting blame;
accept my humble invitation
to eat with me and afterwards,
rested and fed, you can tell me your name.
I fear the gods didn't grant you the ability
to distinguish between grief
and joy.

Odysseus: A Verse Tragedy

ODYSSEUS

    Take my hand old timer,
and pretend I'm an old friend
back again from a twenty-year journey.
Imagine your happiness and cries of joy.
You sacrificed a fattened calf
to celebrate my unhoped-for arrival.
"My most faithful swineherd,"
I would shout, "I'm back, embrace me!
For twenty years I fought
both land and sea, but I triumphed and returned."
Please don't holler; I'll sit quietly,
don't scold me! You asked who I am;
willingly, I'll tell you all my story.

I am Daedalus, the Athenian
whose fame has reached the heavens,
and my brilliant accomplishments
like tall fruit trees reach toward the sun.
Fed up laboring over sunless tombs in Egypt
to expose the mysteries of creation,
I missed the fresh air and light,
the pounding of menacing waves,
the screeching seagulls
and the star-studded heavens.
One spring morning,
shedding my heavy white-hot woven tunic,
weightless, I abandoned,
the dark halls of knowledge
for the blue skies of sun-drenched Greece.

Nikos Kazantzakis

And as I stepped on her holy shores,
my mind blossomed like lilies,
and for the first time all creation
appeared on the calm currents of my mind
smiling deeply satisfied.
I was the first to breathe life and grace
into wood and stone;
the first to pry open
the unwelcoming arms of god and man,
and with patience abolish oppression.
Slowly with patience and love,
I liberated people's divine soul from bestiality.
Minos, that tough imposing master
of the sea, invited me, and I sailed
in a multilevel galley like a king
to world-renowned Knossos of sacred Crete.
I built the magnificent palace
with its coliseums, baths, its vast gardens,
and narrow labyrinthine cellars,
and during those endless years,
I painted the gymnast bulls
and those lovely curly-headed maidens.
I laid my hands upon Astarte's
sacred breasts and braided with snakes
her deific, curly, flowing hair.
Should you ever visit,
you'll witness the worship of the futile efforts
these two mortal hands created.
I yearned for my country, and I sprouted
wings to escape … but your mind old timer
is fraught with hunger. Had I mind to,

Odysseus: A Verse Tragedy

I could unnerve you, and you would scream;
On one of my voyages, I saw Odysseus!

EUMAEUS

Hold your tongue; eat, drink.
I don't need payment in false lies.
You're like all other vagabonds.

ODYSSEUS

I swear I saw him in Calypso's arms,
forsaking both country and wife.
I couldn't help myself; I jumped up
on the bow and cried out in anger:
"Shame on you cunning Odysseus
to allow a woman's love to betray
your country and your obligations!"
"Who abandons Olympos" — he replied —
"to dwell on earth?" And the deep caverns
reverberated with his laughter.
"You can't bluff me; I am too cunning,
and I know what's best for me.
Penelope is old; my son
plays dice with the suitors,
thinks of his future, and forgets his old man.
And if he truly is my son, his heroic
actions upon this earth will prove he's mine.
I intend to abandon my mortal self
and become immortal!" "For shame!" I replied.
"Would you reject the holy soil of Mother Earth,
and bread's tasty savor?"

Nikos Kazantzakis

EUMAEUS

Good for you, you did right, old man.
And how did he respond from the cave?

ODYSSEUS

He shrugged his broad shoulders laughing.

EUMAEUS

Did he remember me?

ODYSSEUS

   Who remembers
slaves?

EUMAEUS

 Isn't that the truth, friend.

ODYSSEUS

    That's no reason
to cry.

EUMAEUS

 What would you have me do, dance?
Incapacitated, he's lost, and we two fine lads

Odysseus: A Verse Tragedy

take his place in the dirt. Sit down
and stop embracing my knees. Let go!

ODYSSEUS

Don't weep. You touch me where it hurts, old timer;
reluctantly learn the truth.
Its two months since I passed by
wealthy Pylos's sandy shores.
A southerly wind was blowing, a storm was brewing,
and from the dark clouds a heavy deluge fell;
everywhere Zeus
cast lightning bolts around us.
Suddenly a lightning flash lay bare
a serene Odysseus in the middle of the sea
holding tight upon a raft,
bracing the storm head-on.
"Odysseus"—I barked—"are you heading home?
Didn't the goddess's bed suit you any longer?"
But he, sporting a silver-white mustache,
bent over the tiller,
stared straight ahead and did not turn.

EUMAEUS

My god, you feed me lies with such craft
that hope baits me once again.

ODYSSEUS

He'll return! It's been only days not months,

since I saw him on a white wave triumphantly approaching
like a soot-black bull devotee.

EUMAEUS

I can't believe it!

ODYSSEUS

   I saw him, look there, can't you see him?
He's back!

EUMAEUS

 I'm frightened; Zeus have mercy!
My mind churns with unhoped-for hope.
Linos, pile wood in the fireplace;
bring a light! A god treads the darkness!

ODYSSEUS

Odysseus is here!

(Linos enters with wood and a lit brand; Odysseus hunches quietly by the doorsill.)

LINOS

   Hey old man you're all tuckered out
and you're dreaming awake.
What frightened you to gawk in the darkness?

Odysseus: A Verse Tragedy

EUMAEUS

Shadows like colossal wings beat about me;
a god entered the hut
and left.

LINOS

    Good God! All this railing about.
Your eyes flutter hither and thither, old man,
and fantasize white sails upon the sea
and shadows near the evening shore.
I'm sick and tired listening to you bicker;
I'm leaving as soon as I start the fire.

EUMAEUS

Are you on an all-nighter again?
You neglect your work and pass the time loafing.

(*Eumaeus, troubled, goes outside circling his hut.*)

ODYSSEUS

Now that the cat is away
the mice will play.

LINOS

      It's our turn!
We'll sit at the master's table

and let his pigs, wine, and bread
feed our ravenous bellies.
The maids will revel with the servants,
and on the boss's wide bed
we'll sleep cuddled in each other's arms.
Fate now shares equally.

ODYSSEUS

But he'll return!

LINOS

    Who?

ODYSSEUS

    The landlord!

LINOS

He's welcome;
I'll put a choker around his neck so he can feed with the pigs.

(*He quickly takes a choker off the wall and puts it around beggar/Odysseus's neck and exits laughing.*)

ODYSSEUS

Hold tight heart!

Odysseus: A Verse Tragedy

It's degrading that a slave's actions should wound
your pride.
Patience; time is on our side.

EUMAEUS (*Returning.*)

Old man, did you see anything? A shadow?

ODYSSEUS

I no longer see shadows.
I just make out two female slaves
on the slope among the rocks
jeering at a limping old man.

EUMAEUS

        Laertes!

ODYSSEUS

          Who?

EUMAEUS

          The master's
father ... why do you jump up?
Your teeth are chattering—are you cold?

Nikos Kazantzakis

ODYSSEUS

Don't hold me back! The master's ...

EUMAEUS

Come near the fireplace,
warm yourself and keep quiet.
Look, I filled your cup with dark wine;
you'll find it comforting; drink up.

(Odysseus grabs the cup and wolfs it down.)

ODYSSEUS

More!

EUMAEUS

My master has good wine...

(He fills his cup again; Odysseus grabs the cup and empties it on the ground.)

ODYSSEUS

That's how I want my dark blood spilled,
if at the right moment
I fail to act.

Odysseus: A Verse Tragedy

EUMAEUS

    What are you mumbling about, old timer?
I think you're drunk.

ODYSSEUS

               The master!
That fearful, awesome, glorious master
whose upright man-slaughtering spear
loomed like a ship's mast
in the hands of good-for-nothing mortals.
And in his wild imaginings
when he jumped up to dance, the lyre
bounced like a living being in the player's hands.
Now he bides his time crawling in the dirt
while his flesh decays …
                    Damn
the gods and their mortal gifts!

EUMAEUS

Don't swear; to be young is priceless.
A thousand obstacles and mockeries
old timer, couldn't pay
for such great joy.
Leaving? Careful! Don't dare raise a finger;
these maids are no longer slaves but ladies.

ODYSSEUS

Bear up heart; hush!

Nikos Kazantzakis

EUMAEUS

                      His eyes drip blood,
and the white mud-smeared beard
turns crimson ...

ODYSSEUS

                      Yes, they have good faces,
but as for brains? Bitches,
the day will come to hang you in the courtyard.

EUMAEUS

Keep quiet, I tell you,
they're overseen by powerful benefactors,
and they don't abide too many excuses.

ODYSSEUS

                      You gods, listen!
Just one more word from me, who keeps untarnished
earth's strict rhythm in my mind.
Keep Fate's scales just,
for how else can man's virtue
ascent striving for Olympos.

(The female slaves Leda and Phaedra enter, shoving Laertes.)

Odysseus: A Verse Tragedy

LEDA

Move along my good lad, lift your feet
and jump over the doorsill.

PHAEDRA

We wove him a funeral wreath, a groom's dowry
with daffodils; under his right arm
he carries a loaf made of honey and nuts
for the three headed freak, Death!

LAERTES

The shroud, my shroud ...

EUMAEUS

                                        Take it!
Your daughter-in-law, God bless her,
sends a gift for your trip of no return—
a sail to open on the sea down under.

(*To Odysseus.*)

For years she fooled the suitors
unweaving in the evening each day's work,
claiming "It's a shame to send unattended
my father-in-law's corpse to Hades.
Don't be in a hurry, lords, let me finish
and Fate will select from among you my husband!"

Nikos Kazantzakis

ODYSSEUS

Now?

EUMAEUS

    She's tired of deceiving ...
but it's a disgrace to disclose house secrets to a stranger;
I'll hold my tongue.

ODYSSEUS

Then keep quiet; I don't want to hear anymore.
I heard enough to choke a horse.

LEDA

The divorcee got bored sleeping
without a man's arms around her, old timer;
a woman has no other secrets.

ODYSSEUS

Don't pull him, you hussy, he'll fall!

(*Laertes falls and the maids laugh; Odysseus rushes and lifts him up, but he can't hold back his tears.*)

Shame on you!

Odysseus: A Verse Tragedy

PHAEDRA

>Goodness; the old timer is crying.

ODYSSEUS

Bitches!

(Alarmed, the maids exit.)

EUMAEUS

>Sit down!

ODYSSEUS

>Good God, father!

(Laertes gets up, shaken; Beggar/Odysseus clasps him in his arms.)

LAERTES

Who's that?

ODYSSEUS

>Me! Father, wake up,
rip off the dark cloud
that blurs your thoughts;

Nikos Kazantzakis

let clarity and sanity favor your mind as before,
and let this phrase reach heaven:
"Your son is alive! Do you hear? Your son is alive!"
But my words fall into a bottomless pit.
I saw the wide-ranging man rise
through the waves holding in his mouth
the two-edged sword of Justice.
And once he's here, you'll leap
exultantly into his arms wailing:
"A miracle my son, what joy; a mere lightning bolt
the twenty years you've been away!"
Endless will be your kisses
upon his face and on his head of grey.

EUMAEUS

Listen, you can't warm a dead carcass.

LAERTES

Did you see him?

ODYSSEUS

      There! He's coming to his senses!
Father, he takes great pains to return,
to unburden himself of the debt
a son owes.

LAERTES

      I'm tired ...

Odysseus: A Verse Tragedy

EUMAEUS

        Leave him alone, he's crying!

ODYSSEUS

He was returning triumphant
with a ship load of copper, slaves, and arms;
on the prow stood a god-like man—your son!
In his wide palms the tiller strained;
around him dolphins
and seagulls frolicked joyfully.
The stars pointed the way,
and everything propelled him toward his native land.

LAERTES

Tell me more; he's coming ... There he is!

EUMAEUS

Like a drowned man revived,
he once again comes to life
and feasts his eyes on the sun.
And you, father, resuscitate his mind.

ODYSSEUS

Oh, revered head.
Speak the simple single word that liberates.

Nikos Kazantzakis

EUMAEUS

Quiet; I hear footsteps ...
It must be one of our own, but who? The dogs aren't barking.

(Telemachos appears on the doorstep.)

Oh, light of my eyes!

TELEMACHOS

Great
benefactress and protectress Athena,
praise be to my faithful swineherd,
who rescues me from the shameful trap,
set by the shifty suitors.
I come, grandfather, to embrace your knees.
Greetings to your loyal, warm hearth Eumaeus.

EUMAEUS

Oh, dear light,
my old eyes have run dry crying,
convinced they would never see you again.
I must be dreaming; perhaps a deceptive god
has taken possession of your handsome form.
How you matured. The sea has scorched your skin.
You sport the face of a man,
and in looks and height you resemble
your godlike father. It's time now, my son,

to grasp hold of the renowned spear
and disperse the carrion crows from
the broad tree of your exalted race.

ODYSSEUS

Steady strong heart, I must stand up.
My child!

TELEMACHOS

   Who calls? Oh, it's you stranger
resting beside this inviting fireplace.
I believe you merit my highest regards. Pardon me,
old man, you seem to be a stranger.
Why do you smile?

EUMAEUS

              Forgive him, Telemachos;
he's a bit tipsy.
He cries and then he laughs;
his wits are under the influence of the wine.
By his side, your grandfather in his troubled sleep
calls on old deserted seashores and cries.
Only I stay awake and wait.
Enlighten my heart, my child,
and tell me the truth: Is he alive?
What news from Sparta, son? Don't hold back;
what do you have to say, life or death?

Nikos Kazantzakis

TELEMACHOS

Perhaps the famous deem us royalty
and call us guiding bulls
among the infinite herds of mankind.
But ask me, who sailed the world's seas
and wrapped my mind around
wonders that foreign lands display.
I passed through mountains and forests,
and our horses grew weary traversing plains.
I beheld exotic women and myriad
rivers, birds, beasts, and trees,
which weigh on me when brought to mind.
I, a neophyte, was amazed
and left speechless in Sparta
gazing upon circles of towering levees.
I crossed ironclad doors
and breathless climbed
the broad royal hill to reach
the palace of world-renowned Menelaos.
My eyes marveled at the sight, my swineherd.
Pure gold the upper floors, the cellars
and the massive heavy palace doors, and passing
through them
thousands of heavily burdened slaves
like ants coming and going night and day.
To subdue my restless, stupefied heart
I exclaimed, "Telemachos, look upon
this glory and wealth with ease;
don't gape like a country bumpkin!"
Privileged, I crossed the bronze
thresholds, my tranquil face

reflected in the glistening bronze.
I moved along the path
and, arriving at the palace, I knocked unflinchingly,
elated at the large historic lintel above me:
a swan spreading its all-white
ivory wings of love,
alighting on light blue waters to embrace
Leda's sun bronzed body.

Two forty-year-old slaves jumped to their feet
to open for me the double doors
with thick gold-plated doorknobs.
And I focused my eyes on treasures
spread before me like the seashore.
Reclining on a royal throne like Zeus,
the semi-god Menelaos, euphoric,
accompanied by song, lyre, and drum;
on a chair opposite a revered chanter,
his hair intertwined with fresh vineyard vines,
sang of Helen's beauty,
which caused the fall of Troy.
Two young maidens among the gleaming columns
danced sprightly as thick blue shells
quivered on their necks,
and their flowing hair lashed their shoulders.
Behind a pale youth, an elderly man leaning against a pillar
performed melodically on a lithesome flute. Suddenly ...

EUMAEUS

I'm out of breath, I tremble ...

Nikos Kazantzakis

TELEMACHOS

>Hush,
don't tremble. The golden doors
of the women's quarters opened, and I beheld
enter the tranquil floral scent of Helen.
My heart went limp; she appeared a goddess
in stature, form, and beauty.

EUMAEUS

A curse on witless beauty!
Cursed be the hour that provoked
such a blossom among the reeds of Eurotas.

TELEMACHOS

Don't blaspheme, father. Before me
she seemed tall, mature, and fair,
like the taste of ripe mellow fruit,
and with a cheerful jolt my heart divined
that life is not man's greatest blessing,
as once I thought.
You watch her calmly open like a flower
and one's hardships melt away, and I burst out,
"such beauty I never hoped to see!"

EUMAEUS

I'm anxious to hear about your father!

Odysseus: A Verse Tragedy

TELEMACHOS

Slowly, she raised her eyes and said,
"I sense from a distance that before me
stands the son of well-intentioned Odysseus.
His goodly body, his height, his faithless eyes,
his convoluted step, which strides
the earth as on a ship.
Bless the tree of life, for each leaf
that falls sprouts another."
She spoke and her smile spread
like the sun and lit both earth and sky.
Glory to youth that perished for your cause,
and triple my father's glory, who sought
to carry you away by trickery. In the fathomless waves
his memory will shine forth like a star.

EUMAEUS

Oh god, my good master is lost forever!

TELEMACHOS

Don't whine; Odysseus has become the subject of songs.
Stalwart at the stern, tiller in hand,
sails lowered, he anchors
in the deep blue waters of Memory.
The lyre immortalizes his eternal name
at the tables of nobles.
I pray the gods grant me
the same fate as his.

Nikos Kazantzakis

ODYSSEUS

They believe that my heart like a barren grapevine
will never bear fruit again;
yet dark curly grapes
of greed and joy burst forth.
A thousand welcomes to you my only son.

EUMAEUS

Master and lord.
If only I were your spear or sword,
your faithful dog,
to scale your pyre and breathe my final breath
at your hallowed feet.

TELEMACHOS *(Addressing Odysseus.)*

It's not becoming to rejoice in lamentation.
You must pay tribute to my ancestral gods.

ODYSSEUS

I laugh to catch my breath. I have a pressing
urge to embrace all three of you
and yet I hold back.

TELEMACHOS

            My rage,
I keep in check. I feel
profound grief for you, ill-fated.

Odysseus: A Verse Tragedy

EUMAEUS

Oh, master, you're lost,
and leave your home in ruins.
Your eagle plume falls on earth
and no longer casts a shadow,
a shield for your son, your wife, and me,
and a dread to others.
What avenger will appear
to bend the great bow?
Undoubtedly your choice
Fate is always best.

TELEMACHOS

Stop your laments my good man;
only songs become his grave.
I ask, have you no respect for youth?
Even if the old man is gone,
I take his place to fight in Greece;
I reach to clasp the spear
from his lifeless hands and cast it
with his blessing beyond
his furthest aim!

ODYSSEUS

           Triple the glory
for him who, before he dies,
attains a worthy son to snatch from his palms
his sturdy spear for heroic deeds.

Nikos Kazantzakis

I too would like my golden years
pillaged by sons with strength and honor.

EUMAEUS

Did you mourn his death, my son?

TELEMACHOS

I paid a son's dues to his father.
Into the enchanted wine
Helen's lily hand cast an herb
and at once soothed my mind
and pacified my heart;
her voice like water refreshed my soul,
"Have no regrets; it's time brave lads
to reap the immortal gifts of heroes
and have the earth reverberate your names.
Come out from under your famous father's shadow
and enter the spotlight on your own.
Like an oak that draws its power from the earth
and impedes another's growth,
your father suckles Ithaca.
Now the playing field remains open
to allow your skill to share the plunder."
She took me by the hand
and aroused a desire in me
to reach and excel my father.

ODYSSEUS

Yet you abandon your life to the suitors

by refusing to lift your head.
They circle your mother like hounds,
while you anxiously search the sea
waiting for an old man's hands to save you.
Do you want to follow him? Pick up his spear
and head for the palace for revenge.
Were he ever to return,
your island would quake with fear,
and like deer, the suitors would cringe
at a lion's scent near-by.
Then they would pay with dark blood
their shameless disregard for hospitality.
Now they revel like wolves, that make their way
into a sheepfold lacking a shepherd and his hounds.

EUMAEUS

Old man, you change before my eyes; you come alive!
You awake in me past memories
of bliss and daring.

TELEMACHOS

               But how can I take on
so many by myself?

ODYSSEUS

By not counting! Make up your mind and fall
into the fray with gusto and you'll triumph.

Nikos Kazantzakis

TELEMACHOS

And do you think the gods will keep me company?

ODYSSEUS

                         They will
If you succeed! I know them; they always pursue
the victor to feed on remnants
like crows.

EUMAEUS

        My hut quakes!

TELEMACHOS

How your mind shines, old timer, a light, a flame.

ODYSSEUS

Whoever endures and returns
Death's conqueror, my son, grasps
that the seed of freedom is the human heart.
Prepare to go beyond the bounds of mortality.

TELEMACHOS

Yes, just like you, I imagine
my world-renowned father!

Odysseus: A Verse Tragedy

EUMAEUS

                    Should you stand up,
I believe, your head would topple
our roof. Undaunted,
you change moods, laughing and crying but now
like a demanding god you rant and rave.

ODYSSEUS

I can morph into a thousand forms,
an infant, an old man, even
water, fire, and air,
or a great toxic bow that bends
like a viper in the sun and slinks away,
willowy, with a brood, and mad as hell.

EUMAEUS

Who are you? My heart beats out of control.

ODYSSEUS

How you gawk, my shepherd.
I'm not a phantom; I'm alive. Touch me.
My strong lean bones bind me
and inside, my soul dwells like a queen.
In every port I stopped,
I was cunning, a spinner of tales.
I sold worthless merchandise as if gold;

all lies. Can anyone consider real
anything sold by one in rags?
And if you truly think I'm Daedalus,
old man, it's because your mind
is overcome with hunger.
I now disclose to you a great lie.
Stand before me with attention.
I am ... are you uneasy?

EUMAEUS

         Tell me, who are you?

ODYSSEUS

               Odysseus!
There! A lie, man's divine right,
which like Cerberus scares me to death.
An easy victory no longer interests me,
nor do I accept it. Come, now, old timer,
spread a blanket for me in your courtyard.
I overdrank this evening, and I mouthed off
a bit too much.... Old father, I'm going to keep you
close to my heart tonight until I can cope
that my two hands clutch earth.

(Eurycleia enters holding the great bow.)

EURYCLEIA

Oh, I curse the day I was born!

Odysseus: A Verse Tragedy

I'm tired of the light; I pound the door,
on the cool earth, and scream.

EUMAEUS

It seems you bring me more misfortunes.
My eyes cloud over …
what in the darkness glistens in your hands?

TELEMACHOS

My father's bow!

EURYCLEIA

              You're back, my boy.
I bow before you, welcome.
What a sweet comfort to our loneliness.
And the master?

EUMAEUS

   He decays in the ocean's depths.

EURYCLEIA

You think the master would disappear
before reaching home to demand justice?
Not possible, no! He has seven lives,
don't fret. He lives and reigns.

Nikos Kazantzakis

EUMAEUS

He reigns in your deranged mind,
but he no longer casts his shadow upon the earth.

EURYCLEIA

I already see his dark shadow
near the island, mounting
the hill rock by rock. There he is,
entering the courtyard; the dogs are howling.
Who knows whether or not he casts anchor
in one of the island's secluded harbors.
He's cunning, and once he docks,
I know him. He won't openly appear.
First, he'll scout for those loyal
and those laying traps for him.
He won't even open up his heart
to his own son before he firms up the nets
in the twisted workings of his mind.

EUMAEUS

Eurycleia, all is lost
If we place our hopes on blind fate.

ODYSSEUS

Eurycleia! How you aged, my good woman.
Your breasts sag;
your white hair once glistened
like crow's feathers on your wondrous shoulders.

Odysseus: A Verse Tragedy

EURYCLEIA

And who is this fellow again in rags?
These paupers pester my master
like crows over carrion.

TELEMACHOS

Take heed old mother; the bow,
why remove it from its old post?
I ordered that it hang there to guard the house
and not be touched.

EURYCLEIA

What can I say my son?

TELEMACHOS

    Why cry? Did my mother send it? Tell me!

EURYCLEIA

Please don't ask!

TELEMACHOS

    Did my mother send it?

EURYCLEIA

        Yes.

Nikos Kazantzakis

TELEMACHOS

Why? Look me in the eyes!
Does she shudder to see it idle on the wall?
Is the master humiliated by its exposure?

EURYCLEIA

My child, trouble comes from far and near.
I struggle to remain silent,
but out of pity, I hold my tongue.
Last night Fate, through
Aphrodite's godly lips, decreed,
"Take down your husband's bow
and announce a contest to the suitors:
whoever casts an arrow through twelve axe heads
will take you as his wife!"
And now, shepherd, I bring it eagerly
to you to rub down with fat and make it pliable.

EUMAEUS

My good master, you dropped out of sight, and everyone
has deserted you... hey you, be quiet; what are you
groaning about?

ODYSSEUS

I'm going to speak if it kills me!
Swineherd, you, an aged man,
who with clenched fists thrash the earth,

and yearn for an open grave,
grasp the meaning of my words.
What a bewildering, pretentious thing is fame,
which openly sweeps through villages and lands
offering herself to every passer-by,
giving birth to hordes of bastards.
Penelope was renowned and revered
throughout this dismal earth.
Bent over her home's hallowed hearth,
we imagined her faithful, preserving the sacred flame
and listening in the far distance to the sea,
weeping for her welfare.
With raised hands, we prayed,
"Grant the same to me, oh Zeus
that my hearth be pure that I may leave
behind such a vigilant wife in my house."
Immortals hear me…. Oh, forget it!
Words lack meat and blood,
and gods are hungry
for chunky thighs wrapped in fat.

TELEMACHOS

Fate divulges against my will
my home's innermost secrets.
Treat them with reverence, stranger.
I'm the only one who has the right to reveal them.

EURYCLEIA

Telemachos, it's about time you show

Nikos Kazantzakis

whose son you are ...
What's on your mind?

EUMAEUS

                  Be quiet! I dread
your fixed unbending stare, my boy.

TELEMACHOS

Enough, old man. On my shoulders,
I feel the dead man's weight;
it's time to stand on my own two feet
and carry my own weight.
Just as he too sought freedom,
I follow in his footsteps.

ODYSSEUS

                  So, what do you intend?
Bend your father's bow
before your parental doorstep and shout,
"Is this how you carry away Odysseus's widow?"

TELEMACHOS

The gods gave me a mind to judge
what I'm capable of;
do it right, and you come out a winner.

Odysseus: A Verse Tragedy

ODYSSEUS

Speak clearly, don't beat around the bush.

TELEMACHOS

          Let Fate choose
her new husband, and I swear
her dowry will be returned intact.
Why govern my life any longer?

ODYSSEUS

What a waste of Helen's words.
Virtuous deeds burst into bloom
in grueling deep ravines, but our youth is cautious.
What if your illustrious father lives?

TELEMACHOS

          If alive,
together like a lion and its cub,
we would engage the enemy;
but look who now remains faithful.

ODYSSEUS

          Forget them!
Better on one's own. I never
placed much faith on supporters,
but relied on mind and bow.

Nikos Kazantzakis

(Grabbing the bow from the old woman's hands.)

Bow, were you a dog, you would be rabid.
Eumaeus, I order you to harness it
with bull-like strength lest overuse shatter it.

TELEMACHOS

You sound like a fortune teller ...

EUMAEUS

       No, not a fortune teller, no ...
But you're not Daedalus.

ODYSSEUS

    You're right, I'm not.

EUMAEUS

You resemble ...

EURYCLEIA

    Yes, the look, the height, the shoulders ...

ODYSSEUS *(Breaking out in laughter.)*

Like putty in my hands,

Odysseus: A Verse Tragedy

I shape and reshape the mind of man
and imbue it with my indomitable spirit.

I am the rhapsode, the glory of the Argives,
whom the great Agamemnon trusted
to guard his faithless wife.
The fool! From her I learned
the countless deficiencies of mortals ...
And when the great leader stood victorious
before his palace's indifferent door,
I bowed before him, and taking his massive hands in mine,
secretly paid my respects and entreated him,
"General, hold your longing and aim
to bludgeon with your solemn mind
the cunning viper that lurks before you.
Commander, a bloody bath awaits
your exulted undefeated body!"
And the pale prophetess Cassandra,
death's most precious flower,
forsaken by god, groaned at his feet.
But who can vanquish Fate? Like a bull,
he bellows in the bath and is slaughtered.
And I said, "I curse the earth, the sun,
the merciless and indifferent gods,
who on Olympos eat and drink,
without respect for mortal bearing,
and praise Injustice on their knees."

EURYCLEIA

I'm appalled at all the cursing!

Nikos Kazantzakis

TELEMACHOS

Tell us more!

ODYSSEUS

And the sky reverberated, but I laughed.
"Hey Zeus, debaucher of our women" —
I shouted — "what are you thundering about? I stripped
and exposed you as nothing more than a scarecrow
in space,
and like a proprietor I enter without fear
to harvest earth's wide orchard."

TELEMACHOS

And you're not afraid?

ODYSSEUS

Of whom? My struggles made me
bold and taught me, my boy,
to rely only on myself and endure.
Words are intrepid but only deeds
count. Get to know the human heart.
They're laughing, do you hear? They party
with your household maids, and the suitors mock you …
What are you waiting for? If your father isn't within you,
where do you think he is?
Can you bend his mighty bow?
Then Odysseus has arrived.

Odysseus: A Verse Tragedy

If you can't, he hasn't come,
and I assure you, he never will.

EUMAEUS

    Where are you going?

TELEMACHOS

                      Home!
Your words have scorched my brain,
and shame reddens my cheeks.
I'll attack; God be my witness.
I'll get rid of them openly so people
will praise me and say, "Odysseus
sprouts new buds
and his son doesn't shame his famous father."

EUMAEUS

Don't be in a hurry; allow the deed
to ripen in your mind and give it time to fall
like a mellow fig from its bough.
I despise whoever is quick to act.

ODYSSEUS

And I despise the one who waits forever.

Nikos Kazantzakis

EUMAEUS

Old timer, don't be so quick to offer advice
to a young boy; beware the dangers.

ODYSSEUS

I take into account only a man's strength
and his many private obligations.

TELEMACHOS

What should I do? My blood boils
hot and pure; I learned from my father
to be a harsh master to my anger.

EURYCLEIA

How I admire your selfish youth.
I see in you your father,
when as a beardless youth, with his companions,
he rigged a multi-tiered boat
to abduct the virtuous Penelope ...

EUMAEUS

I'd like to see you inherit his manhood
but even more, if you can, his cunning.

Odysseus: A Verse Tragedy

TELEMACHOS

As a beggar, I heard, he slipped in Troy
to steal Athena's statue and with cunning
bring Victory to our troops.
No one from the enemy guessed
who wore the tattered clothes.
Only Helen was not deceived; the godlike
woman recognized him but kept silent.
Smiling, she hastily bathed him,
anointed him with scented oils,
laid an opulent linen robe
on his sun-drenched shoulders,
and looking askew at the stolen goddess
on his shoulder, softly and impishly said,
"Quickly, take Victory and leave
and don't forget my greetings, Odysseus,
to the husband I desire."

ODYSSEUS

It's time to put an end to haughty words;
head straight home and slaughter lambs
to Athena to counsel you wisely,
for the mind should always
treat madness in secret and in stealth.

TELEMACHOS

Like a son I kiss your shoulders and your hands.
Come to the palace early in the morning—

assist me in whatever the goddess asks.
An old man's opinion befits the young.
Old timer ...

EURYCLEIA

      He must have fallen asleep,
duped by his dream ... What a mess.

TELEMACHOS

Old chap, I bow before your sainted knees,
and pray that Athena
enlighten your pallid mind
to see in me your son restored.

(*Telemachos and the old woman exit; the swineherd follows them for a short distance.*)

ODYSSEUS

Alone with you, my heart, once again;
hold tight the helm, don't be afraid.
My son hastens to free himself from his father,
and my faithful wife seeks a new playmate
to bear him sons
as if I never existed.
Am I not standing on my own patch of earth?
Ancestors, are you looking down at me?
Somehow, I found foreign lands
more agreeable and friendly.

Odysseus: A Verse Tragedy

     Alas, why abandon the goddess.
What if I did forget my country?
I was living through happier times,
reclining by her side like an endless river
every evening by the sea ...
If only the journey could begin again.
I recall the Sirens' enticing songs,
which, like kisses, rob
the fortunate of their manhood...
In the moonlight their ample breasts
erect like circular
shields of battle ...

For shame, Odysseus! Get over yourself and silence
your memory, the simpering Siren.
With Calypso I could have been immortal
or stay with Circe
and live like a beast. But I held
the tiller steady between two precipices,
focused on humanity's fate.

Lord, I kiss your hands, your feet
your revered head
and tarnished eyes. Bless me father;
let my mind sprout new roots
that I may stand without fear
silently on the threshold of my home.

(Enter Eumaeus.)

Nikos Kazantzakis

EUMAEUS

All sleep. I, sleepless, all night long
lamenting this wretched bow,
which tomorrow will twang a stinging arrow
at my master's heart.
Athena, grant that I witness their deaths
with the courage I presently muster,
and I will sacrifice a gilded yearling heifer
on your temple to satiate your thirst.

How this old timer sways my heart.
Don't lose it, Eumaeus. Don't be afraid;
Patience. Your turn will come.
As long as you're an anvil, bide your time;
when you become a bullet, strike. And keep a log
of what takes place in your memory, good or bad.

Part II

(*Odysseus's palace. Morning, in front of a large paved courtyard with low columns. In the center a high temple, and in front of it a roughly carved wooden multi-breasted statue of Aphrodite. The suitors are lying on bull hides drinking. Maids are hustling back and forth serving wine in tall bronze cups. In the atrium other servants are setting tables.*)

EURYMACHOS

Mischievous, merciless Aphrodite,
ravenous and immortal, be mindful
of all the well-bred young bulls
that I slaughtered in their prime
in your honor, Lady, to quench your hunger.
Recall the rich renowned robes,
I procured to clothe
your revered multi-breasted frame.
On your behalf, I threw Athena to the wind
and smothered the perpetual flame
set at her feet like an eye.
I satiated you with offerings and scents.

Nikos Kazantzakis

Now I supplicate you not as a beggar,
but one requesting payment ... I dealt; now deal.
I sustained you, attend me now if you can.
Recall how I found you famished,
roving like a dog in heat
in these cobwebby courtyards, and I rescued you,
and enthroned you a lady in the palace.
Be mindful that I will cast you out again
in taverns and sleazy harbors,
if in my hour of need
you refuse to champion me.
I'm done; you know my secret.

ANTINOOS

Your cries to the ruthless Lady are in vain,
Eurymachos.
        Fill the tall copper vessels
to the brim with wine, maids,
for a single drop will uncork
the good Penelope's bed tonight.

EURYMACHOS

When will Penelope appear on the balcony like Artemis
holding in her hands the bow?

LEODES

Phemios, fetch your divine lyre
and calm our restless spirits with the mellow

melodies of your disdainful song.
Why lament and remove
the fresh grapevine wreath that graces
your revered wailing brow?

PHEMIOS

I heard a drop of blood fall
warm and heavy on the wedding tables.

LEODES

Brothers, don't laugh. I fear
the singing head that cries.

AGELAOS

(Jumping up agitated.)

Suddenly my heart beats faster.
Today, as prophesied,
the twenty-year cycle comes full circle.
A great shadow falls upon the threshold;
night draws near, and the dogs begin to howl.

EURYMACHOS

Your fears evoke him,
not prophecies.

Nikos Kazantzakis

LEODES

>Our sentry Vigla is late …

ANTINOOS

>Aren't you tired,
Leodes, being told
how forlorn the wave whirls about,
and the earth withholds its dead?

EURYMACHOS

It's a shame the way fear affects us.
Bring out the dancing girls,
and let's get drunk. Ignorance is bliss.
Look how those white ankles gaily tread the earth.

PHEMIOS

Wait, first listen to my dream.

ANTINOOS

Perhaps you dreamed his frothy prow
slicing in the night across your mind?

PHEMIOS

A new day dawned,
and the wedding glasses on the tables

Odysseus: A Verse Tragedy

overflowed with dark wine.
Like wild fire the great celebration
fanned out and spread throughout the palace.
And I, standing in the center, sang
to ignite the spirit in the bridegroom's chest.
Suddenly, Penelope, like an owl,
clasped the circular stairway,
"It's time"—she cried—"for the contest to begin!"
The lyre slips from my hands; I sense
the feathers of a feral raven on my head.
I turn around and imagine the great bow
hissing and leaping like a viper
from its high column, and jumping
on the banquet tables, it begins to dance.
Its searing blue-stone eyes,
blazing, sparkle on its head,
whirling around, slowly, craving blood.
"A snake, Aphrodite"—I shouted—"save me!"
But on the portal, I sight silently standing
a fully armed Athena, her bronze spear
blazing and her dark blue eyes
like untraceable gems
fixed, pure; how they penetrate.
"It must be a dream" I screamed.
Released from sleep, I jump up
like a wild beast in the night,
like Death's ghastly night bird
unashamedly trilling in the courtyard,
and between my eyebrows Apollo's
voice severs like a spear.

AGELAOS

It's Vigla!

LEODES

    Who? My knees buckle.

VIGLA

He's here!

ANTINOOS

    Where did you see him? Speak!

LEODES

                            That's it,
we're lost.

AGELAOS

He's here!

EURYMACHOS

    You're all frightened to death,
and unstrung, and unfocused,
you yearn the throne.
Shame on you. Vigla, I order you

to bolster your heart and tell me: Did you see him
or did your eyes play tricks on you?

VIGLA

I saw him with my own two eyes. Last night
as I was coming down the hill cursing.
Suddenly, on the harbor opposite, I spot
a ship docking late in the evening.
On my belly, like a viper on a rope,
I slide and make out someone jumping
secretly on the sand and hurrying
to the swineherd's hut.
It was getting late, and impossible
to bring you the news.

LEODES

So, what's next?

AGELAOS

                    What else? Welcome him home!
It's embarrassing to fear forever;
it's time to fear no more.

VIGLA

What's going on lads? You're talking
about Odysseus, may he rest in peace;
I'm speaking about Telemachos.

Nikos Kazantzakis

ANTINOOS

Get the hell out, you old hag
before I break your jaw.

EURYMACHOS

Good God, it's humiliating to fear a single man.
You all laugh, but I say it's a waste
to squander away unspent youth.

LEODES

Girls, start dancing and let the earth bloom
to lighten our heavy hearts;
let our shame fade away in a single kiss.

EURYMACHOS

Phemios, your heart tumbles
into a bottomless pit; strum your lyre cheerfully.
What must be not even God can change.

PHEMIOS

If he's fated to arrive, then he's welcome.
Place the lyre in my hands
to strum like a spear of battle.
Bring me a vine leaf garland,
and let its dew freshen my brow.
My heart yearns again; like a falcon
my soul glides and clasps my head.

A cricket sits on my thought's
highest bough and chirps
blissfully on death's gateway.

(He plays the lyre; the women dance and sing unhurriedly around him.)

CHORUS

> A golden ornament on an olive tree
> I place
> and on all things from above
> I gaze.
> I knead what's sown,
> cultivate what is grown
> and with a lot of chirping
> I gather by reaping.
> A drop of dew I suspend
> on a weed
> and a bit of honey
> on a fig!

(At that very moment, impoverished and tattered, the beggar/Odysseus enters leaning on the door's column. Behind him follows Eumaeus who moves toward a table and places the bow in the center. All are caught unawares, and the chorus stops abruptly.)

EUMAEUS

I drink to the health of one and all.

Nikos Kazantzakis

PHEMIOS

                Oh, oh! I better leave.

EURYMACHOS

Why are you looking at the door,
and sniffing at the old man like a bloodhound?

PHEMIOS

                    My nostrils
smell human meat from all sides.

AGELAOS

The pig man laces our wine
with wormwood poison, my brothers!

KTESIPPOS

(Tossing a bone at Odysseus's head.)

What are you babbling about, old man? Eat!

EUMAEUS

Take pity on his white whiskers, Ktesippos;
keep in mind that you too have a master.

Odysseus: A Verse Tragedy

KTESIPPOS

We don't need any tears today; songs
and roasted lamb go better at weddings.

EUMAEUS

Just as you mocked the stranger,
may the Immortals consent
that your wedding plans go askew.
Zeus
father, subdue their insolence
when they are shamelessly overcome
under the master's bow.

ANTINOOS

                Know that Immortals listen
only to the prayers of men of action.

KTESIPPOS *(To Odysseus.)*

What are you looking at and clenching your teeth?
You sniff around the columns and tables,
and your nostrils are astir like a dog's;
bark, so we can see how you yap.

(Enraged, he leaps and hits him.)

Nikos Kazantzakis

EUMAEUS

Immortals, where are you? Show yourselves;
this is the moment to show people
compassion.

ANTINOOS

      Look at that, the swineherd raises his hands
with longing to the heavens in supplication
and awaits a miracle.

EUMAEUS

What pity that the gods govern with laws
both the heartless and the unholy,
and humiliate the innocent.

(Melantho enters running and places her water jug on the threshold.)

MELANTHO

Hit him! Don't feel sorry for him.
He fancies secret friends in the palace
and without shame he coerces and threatens.
How can I explain, when I'm still shaken?
As I was returning with my water jug, I saw
the beggar stealthily climbing
over the threshold and eyeing fearfully
the door, the courtyard, and the tables.

Suddenly, I saw Argos jump up
from a corner of the dung heap
panting, sniff the air,
and suddenly jump on the stranger
very animated, shaking his tail.
Fully absorbed, he licked his grimy feet
and nuzzled up to him
with tears pouring hard and fast.
Spinning around, the old timer bent over
and grabbed Argos by the throat ...

PHEMIOS *(Frightfully.)*

       We're lost!

EURYMACHOS

Did he choke him?

MELANTHO

       He strangled him with a passion.

PHEMIOS

A bad sign. I'm leaving!
The doors haven't been bolted yet but will be.

(Telemachos appears among the columns.)

Nikos Kazantzakis

TELEMACHOS

You shameless suitors, I've returned alive,
 strong from my journey,
and I call on Athena to my side
to shake the foundations of my house.

ANTINOOS

You puff up like a viper,
but I'm going to deflate you.

AGELAOS

Brothers wait; this stranger,
like Death, disrupts our feasting.
Hey, Menytes, rough him
up a bit.

MENYTES

      Take that!

ANTINOOS

      Look at those two deadbeats
go at each other. The old timer is enraged
and his teeth are clenched; the whites
of his eyes are spinning.

AGELAOS

                He's
throwing off his rags.

ANTINOOS

              Would you look at those thighs!
Those shoulders!

EURYMACHOS

              I think Menytes
is leaving us for Tartarus unannounced.

ANTINOOS

You might say it brings Odysseus to mind
offering a slaughtered animal for his wife's wedding.

EURYMACHOS

Congratulations, old timer;
Menytes's jaw is shattered,
and his nostrils spout dark blood.

ANTINOOS

Old timer, why do rags
conceal your stately body? You appear

like a robust bull mating with a heifer
in a luxuriant meadow.
My heart tells me to anoint you with oil
and go toe to toe; you're worthy of my time.

AGELAOS

You don't appear a beggar; perhaps a trader.
The chest, the thighs, and your shoulders
point to a hardened sailor.

TELEMACHOS

                Remove
the corpse, and may the immortals
visit the same fate on all the lawless.

(They remove Menytes's corpse. Telemachos turns covertly to Odysseus.)

Listen stranger; in a dream last night
Athena came to me rejoicing, "Stay
strong"—she counseled—"keep your wits about you
and your eyes fixed on the old man;
whatever he beckons, carry out with respect.
He justly holds the fate of your palace
in his massive hands."

ODYSSEUS

That's fine; don't be in a rush; I'll signal.

Odysseus: A Verse Tragedy

PHEMIOS

(Noticing the two whispering.)

Listen to what I'm about to say, you weighty suitors.
This stranger is a suspicious prophet.
Look at him; he doesn't speak but prowls around
like a boar pursued by dogs.
He has bloodshot eyes. The sun
has dimmed, and I hear wings on my right.

(Unsettled, the suitors amble about beggar/Odysseus, who breaks out laughing.)

ODYSSEUS

Haughty suitors you need not fear
malicious earths' mourning flowers.
So much suffering sits on my heart
that my lips have forgotten the cordial
smile that pampers nobles;
since I cannot speak, I scream!

ANTINOOS

Set weeping aside, old timer, and confess
why you traverse the world's harbors?

ODYSSEUS

For the cursed belly

Nikos Kazantzakis

armed ships brave the seas,
and for my belly I too have returned
to fall before your feet. I beg you place in my hands
some bread and meat to assuage my hunger.
Pity me, Antinoos, don't send me away.
As a great king on public view,
you must have learned to give
graciously. Now I am confined
in my mind like an old dream.
I was deemed thrice blessed
and possessed a rich home that echoed
with the laughter of my cherished child.
I held him in my arms and prayed,
"My child may you prosper and become
in archery and knowledge superior to me."
And as he crawled upon the dirt,
sweet were the first words he babbled,
which fill with joy man's fateful heart.
Now my life is over, ladened
on a freighter sailing near Cyprus;
my son, captured by pirates, is a slave
and God only knows in what noble's bed
my wife lies and gives birth to worthy
sons, a joy to his old age.

(Antinoos kicks him; beggar/Odysseus loses his balance and almost falls.)

ANTINOOS

Misfortune and weeping don't concern me;

Odysseus: A Verse Tragedy

I have only one thing on my mind,
to execute this evening twelve obstacles[1]
and occupy Odysseus's bed.

ODYSSEUS

It's true, gods never bestow their gifts
upon people out of the blue. You possess
a noble figure and curly hair
that could adorn Apollo's head,
but in your royal chest
you have little insight, which like a worm gnaws and decays
the divine fruit of your admirable youth.

TELEMACHOS

Antinoos, I don't want anyone abusing
the stranger in my house. You tread uncivilly
on god's laws, and you will account to me.

ANTINOOS

Listen you popinjay, I'm going to grab you
by the neck and slam you on the ground
like an octopus until your tentacles are paralyzed.
I'll pound you on the flagstones until you're liquefied.

---

[1] Antinoos must shoot an arrow through twelve ax heads in order to win the hand of Penelope.

Nikos Kazantzakis

KTESIPPOS

You poked around the seas to rake up
the footprints of your hated father,
but he died; mourn him, and don't be humiliated
by the fat cattle he pillaged on his travels.

AGELAOS

Your father was never a lofty lion
but rather a wily fox.
To triumph he even wore rags
demeaning his manhood and stealthily,
with his mind askew, he found ways
to outsmart victory with cunning.

ODYSSEUS

(Soliloquizes.)

Heart, my sturdy heart, I marvel at
the way you hold the reins and race
like a silent arrow toward your objective.
Good Lord, I might even be a god!

TELEMACHOS

Odysseus's renown reaches heaven.
In thought and in battle, he is the very best.
His words like winter snowflakes
fall thick and soft, and his mind

Odysseus: A Verse Tragedy

functions like that of Zeus.
Crouched in the wooden horse
with lamenting captains all in doubt,
surrounded by a dense clutter of teeming Trojans,
only my father, undaunted,
smiled; what nerves of steel,
impervious to the obliteration of Troy.

ODYSSEUS

My boy, fortunate is the father exalted
suddenly in his old age to such heights
and held lofty in his son's esteem;
immortal is one who leaves behind such offspring.

ANTINOOS

(Throwing him a bone.)

Here sink your teeth in this and scram
to your admirer to be mourned a savior.

PHEMIOS

Alas, Fate! Where do you cast us?
I see Athena standing erect
in the middle of the courtyard bearing
her spear in the darkening air.
She caught sight of us and in terrifying silence
shakes threateningly her armored head…
There, she approaches the bronze planks
of the threshold and the black columns blaze.

Nikos Kazantzakis

LEODES

Open the door!

EURYMACHOS

      I drink to your health,
world-renowned Odysseus, whether you repine
among white waves or loiter on land.
Great phantom can you hear me? Welcome.

PHEMIOS

(*He crawls and grabs hold of beggar/Odysseus's feet.*)

Take pity on us; don't play
so mercilessly the game of death.
Get it over with! Why delay? What are you waiting for?
Not a soul remains, shut the doors;
we are all ensnared in your fisherman's net.

EURYMACHOS

Phemios, speak like a man!

LEODES

      My pale body
trembles apprehending death.

Odysseus: A Verse Tragedy

ODYSSEUS

How disgraceful! What do you fear?
Why embrace my knees, poet? I'm just a beggar
circulating among these nobles' tables,
expecting a bite to eat.
Forgive me, Antinoos, for having begged
touching your lordly body with these dirty hands.
In spite of my meddling ploys,
I bow before your feet.
Would you prefer me to dance with swords?
To close my mouth and arch my body,
until it touches the soles of my feet?
I can even fight a bull
by taking hold of its horns, with skill
vault on its back,
and with ease jump on the ground.
But you might get a bigger kick
If I danced Persephone's dance naked
as is popular in my native land.
Rejoicing, we dance upon the graves,
treading on spring time pastures.

EURYMACHOS

Phemios pick up your lyre
and accompany his dance of death.

ODYSSEUS

                Recall the song

of heroes building a castle
to escape their end?
Whatever in the world oh god befell ...

PHEMIOS

Yes, I do; but oh, god, a knot
on my supple throat chokes me.

ODYSSEUS

Phemios! Whoever gets up to dance, must dance.

(Phemios sings; Odysseus pulls off his clothes and dances.)

PHEMIOS

Whatever, oh, God befell those heroes,
who built an iron castle to keep Death at bay?
They built it out of iron and locked themselves in,
but Death appeared a rider on the ley.
Dark was he, dark his dress, and dark his steed;
dark the bloodhounds and dark the entire scene.

(Phemios stops and cries.)

EURYMACHOS

Continue poet, don't slack off;
youth need not fear Death;
manly and valiant is he,
and we welcome him to our feast.

Odysseus: A Verse Tragedy

ODYSSEUS

Hey old singer of fairy tales
do you think with lays and tears
you can cheat Fate into submission?
Earth like a thirsty cesspool
wolfs down her children, both beasts and men.

ANTINOOS

Sing, lest I loosen your throat
with my sword. Among us, why fear?

PHEMIOS

He greets them from afar, and approaching says,
"I salute you lads!" "Greetings Death,
wherefrom do you come and whither do you go?"
"My lads, I'm here to receive your souls."
"We, men of courage, refuse to yield our souls."
Their words were newly made and misfortune had yet to come,
a tremor ensued, and the castle fell from view,
a small cloud descended upon the heroes,
their eyes closed, and their world from them flew.

(Phemios cries. Penelope appears on the top step; she sees beggar/Odysseus dancing in the nude. Beggar/Odysseus turns and sees Penelope; embarrassed he wraps his rags around him and leans against a column.)

Nikos Kazantzakis

PENELOPE

You seem one with insight, old man, and yet
you neglect to respect your age,
dancing naked before young men.
There are many ways for a mortal
to earn his bread; I think it a disgrace
to go to such lengths unnecessarily.
And now, if you desire, I'll order the maids
to treat you to some sweet wine and meat.

ODYSSEUS

If you are Penelope's heavenly
form, my eyes are overjoyed.
I journeyed to many lands and towns,
and had my fill of beautiful women,
but now like a neophyte, I'm overwhelmed
by longing. I tremble sweetly before you
my lady.

PENELOPE

    Tell me did you see Helen of Sparta?
She must be more beautiful than me.
The slut; the men she buried.
And yet her fame is world renowned,
and she remains an object of desire.

Odysseus: A Verse Tragedy

ODYSSEUS

                Your fame,
lady, surpasses reckless Helen's.
The earth that nurtures you rejoices
like soil sprouting an all-white lily.
You're like one of the columns in your husband's
palace, which, upright, holds up the ceiling.
You stand sleepless like a lamp and light up
with patience both the upper and lower stories.
You administer with care animals, slaves,
the cooking, and measure out each task.
Your home functions blissfully
to the cadence of the loom, and you tell the maids,
hoping to retrace your good husband,
"I dreamed last night of a scarlet robe.
He romps with wealthy rakes and sways,
and like a god he dons assorted robes.
In the market place, he's admired by all the nobles
he meets in conversation
because, I'm told, red denotes quick of mind!"
And now that I see before me that heavenly wonder
of a wife, I shout, "blessed be the earth
that bore you, lady."

PENELOPE

Immortals hold in contempt too much pride,
and one should live humbly; that, I believe,
is within man's reach, whether rich or poor.
Fate's directive returns me

time and again to that beaten path,
and I don't put money on too many accolades.
I'm not a goddess but a frail mortal.

ODYSSEUS

Are you sure you didn't mistake your heart's longing
for the voice of Fate, my lady?

AGELAOS

                    Old timer,
It's time to move on;
you heard our mistress's good words.
Old man, don't get between the young.

EURYMACHOS

Oh, undying beauty, welcome!
You stand out like a red apple
in the hands of Fate, and we all reach out
trembling, lady, hoping to carry you away.
Immortals, hear my prayer.
I'm not asking for favors, no!
Let whoever among us is the wealthiest,
the noblest, the wisest be the lucky winner.

ANTINOOS

Let the strongest amongst us triumph
and enjoy you to produce together

Odysseus: A Verse Tragedy

royal progeny to populate Greece.

PENELOPE

Your words pierce my heart
like arrows loosed by skilled archers.
How can I, a widow, lift my head
and select through my dark widow's veil
from among such shining celestial stars?
Let Fate's genial face, which sets limits
for both gods and mortals, choose.
Necessity demands it.
But first let's hope for the appearance
of sweet-tempered Aphrodite in our courtyard.

PHEMIOS

Once again like a flame, like a knife,
anxiety sears my lips.
Queen, don't let your illustrious foot
cross the scarlet threshold.

PENELOPE

You're scaring me, Phemios; you mistook
a crow for an evil sign, instead of entrails;
I rest secure in my Memory, content
in the innocence my face reveals.

Nikos Kazantzakis

ANTINOOS

My lady, cross the threshold without fear;
should Death see us, he'll unsettle us.

PHEMIOS

Lady, on the polished threshold,
I see a giant shadow of a man kneeling,
effortlessly swinging a humming bow.

PENELOPE

You bring to mind my exalted husband,
and I shudder at his piercing eyes
severing my bowels and mind.

TELEMACHOS

Within these walls he still lives and reigns.

PENELOPE

Only God sets limits to everything, my son.

(To Beggar/Odysseus.)

And you should pay homage to this house;
don't swagger around like a savage
shaking your scruffy head;
you tread a royal palace and need to show respect.

Odysseus: A Verse Tragedy

ODYSSEUS

I'm in a daze, lady, and the earth
churns like an angry sea under my feet.
What palace do you speak of?
I sight a ship with red sails,
and its rigging chafes my storm-tossed mind.
The cheerful captains are on a spree,
and Death in a rage grabs the tiller.

PENELOPE

Stranger, earlier you were more genial,
now your words flow like poison
and fly like arrows from your mouth.

ODYSSEUS

Lady, for your sake, I take an oath.
In war I was forgiving
and released the warriors and slaves I captured.
"Perhaps a Penelope sits
faithfully on his threshold waiting,"
I pondered, and felt compassion.
And now before you in your home,
lady, I curse human stock.
Yet mulling over the mortal heart,
I judge human decency with sympathy.
Beautiful as you are, it's a pity
to wait so many years for a husband.
I understand faithfulness is a virtue,

but should respond to the needs of passion.
Imagine how many encircling suitors
desire you, my lady; whisper in Aphrodite's
ear the one you favor.
You know her empathy, she'll listen.
If only my strength was as once it used to be
in my early reckless youth, I would seize hold of
that deadly bow in my own hands.

PENELOPE *(Smiling.)*

You're too old! Make room for younger men.
Don't stand in my way; what is to be will be.
We're all slaves to Fate.

ODYSSEUS *(To himself.)*

       Freedom,
how you overflow like a holy spring
from within Necessity's dark bowels
to refresh my idle mind.

EUMAEUS

It's time my queen; the twelve ax heads
stand ready and waiting.
Hand over the bow to the suitors.

PENELOPE

First, let the goddess's hand bless it.

Odysseus: A Verse Tragedy

Good Aphrodite set your divine hands
on blind Fate and guide her.
You know I didn't renege on my promise
when my good husband left
for those distant accursed shores.
Taking hold of my hand at the threshold,
he pronounced, "Many of us, wife, will be lost
and will never again return to our country
because our enemies are known for gallantry
and are expert spearmen and horsemen.
Your main preoccupation should be my home;
attend my aging parents with care.
Know that caring for my ancestors
you're serving me although absent.
And in time when a beard's shadow
on our son's face begins to show,
you can abandon my household
and marry whomever meets your eye.
It would be offensive, youthful and beautiful
as you will be, to wilt away for me,
for by then I will have forsaken earth,
decaying in ocean's soggy depths.
Immortals loathe an uncultivated field,
which unseeded, fallow, and infertile turns to thorns."
These were Odysseus's final instructions,
as he took leave of his unfortunate wife.
And I resolved to pine for him
fully veiled in my widow's isolation,
focused on cherishing my son
until, a full bearded man at last,

Nikos Kazantzakis

he turned his attention to young maids.
But I swear that I never
set my eyes on anyone else
nor any soul inferior to my husband's;
his great shadow always towered over me.
Now the gods command and I obey.
Fate, do not come to me blind and sullen,
but bring along Aphrodite as a chaperone
to select for me a handsome lad,
the gods' luck of the draw,
to mount my high queenly bed.

THE FEMALE DANCERS

High above your wooly
heads, Justice
spreads her wings
and fills the air with chimes
—greetings Father War—
Victory!

Happy the sturdy arm
that bends the heavy bow
and lops off the flower
the widow nursed for years.
Happy the youth exalted
by Fate.

Like a bull,
you befriend the bold, Lord;
exalt the one

at an auspicious table whose sharp teeth
take a bite out of life
as if an apple.

Like a flame thrower on a steed,
you incite one's youth.
To our right, God;
to the left leaps Death, and undeviating,
we charge fearlessly for honor's
destiny.

Father War, rage
and fear encompass us;
our hearts beat rapidly
and standing erect with bloody feet,
point at the narrow ax head,
Victory!

ODYSSEUS

Hold still my heart; never before
have you felt such beastly agony.

TELEMACHOS *(Whispering.)*

            Old timer, enough at last;
it's time to open your mouth
and signal the slaughter.

Nikos Kazantzakis

ODYSSEUS

It's not time yet.
Wait!

TELEMACHOS

Till when?

ODYSSEUS

Until I signal.

TELEMACHOS

You order me around too much.

ODYSSEUS

God speaks, commands,
and secretly battles in my brain.
Respectfully, I listen and do his bidding.
Attend to those about to die while they exalt
your mother, and like bulls drag them
to the nets I've set in our courtyard.
Don't address me privately; they'll see us; go!

TELEMACHOS

Onward suitors, the prize is a worthy one.
Who can match my mother's wealth,

Odysseus: A Verse Tragedy

character, skill, and intellect?
But it's not right for me to laud
her virtues.

PHEMIOS

    The gallant forms before me
are restless in the oppressive light
of death ... I take joy
in this futile celebration of life.

LEODES

I'm aware you serve only
the powerful, Aphrodite; nevertheless,
the unexpected is attainable. I, too,
although frail, will take a turn at the heavy bow.
I know on earth hope springs eternal.

PENELOPE

Woe to him who hangs his luck
on miracles. Bend the bow, it's worth
whatever your strength can accomplish.

LEODES

But it's impossible to bend.

AGELAOS

                Your lily-white hands

should not toughen in labor;
in bed they must delicately play
the peaceful games of love.

ANTINOOS

Put down the bow, my brave one;
Eurymachos, only the two of us
can tame victory like a mare.

ODYSSEUS *(Privately.)*

Merciful Athena, lightning-eyed.
I sense your strong presence,
and sense in the air your virgin frame;
are you listening? I need a clear sign.

(Loud thunder. A mill woman appears from the colonnade.)

FIRST MILL WOMAN

Father Zeus, you send a powerful sign,
a thunderclap on our defiled earth.
They violate our master's wife;
but you, vigilant thunderclap, grind
your thunderbolt on lawless heads.

SECOND MILL WOMAN

(She also enters from the colonnade and raises her hands.)

Odysseus: A Verse Tragedy

Athena, if I could only grind their heads.
The millstone has broken my back;
It's time for this bitter wheat
to turn into fresh loaves
that slaves might also eat.

THIRD MILL WOMAN

        Where are you master?
Odysseus, they're taking your wife.

ODYSSEUS

Abettor, I sense a spirit
nudging me.

EURYCLEIA

(*Enters the front door, shakes her fists at the sky.*)

    A thunderclap; it's Odysseus's mount.
Welcome a thousand times to the courtyard
you recognize and neigh.

ODYSSEUS

Oh, unhappy forefathers, who from deep
within the earth supply the source of our awe-
inspiring roots.
Not from above, but from below,
I sense the thunderbolt's aggression.

Nikos Kazantzakis

TELEMACHOS

(*Privately to Odysseus.*)

Did you hear the thunder? A good sign!
I no longer set limits to my strength.

ODYSSEUS

Patience!

TELEMACHOS

    I'm tired of waiting!

ODYSSEUS

    What's your rush?

TELEMACHOS

I'm no longer satisfied bending to an old man's whims.

ODYSSEUS

Son!

Odysseus: A Verse Tragedy

TELEMACHOS

    Who is it?

ODYSSEUS

    It's me, son!

TELEMACHOS

    Who?

ODYSSEUS

Telemachos, I'm back. Bolster your heart,
brace your knees lest they buckle;
let your eyes behold Odysseus.

TELEMACHOS

Father!

(*He goes to hug him; the suitors are watching. Odysseus pushes him back.*)

ODYSSEUS

    Stand back!
Be a man and hold your joy; Don't shout!

Nikos Kazantzakis

PHEMIOS

Alas, Athena has boggled your minds
and sealed your eyes in hoar frost.
Oh, my brave lads, black night shrouds
your knees, hips, chests,
sight, and curly hair.
The wailing has begun, red cords
wind around your fleshy necks;
the walls, rafters, and thresholds
dredge up sounds and seep black blood.

AGELAOS

Don't try to hamstring us, Phemios.
If you're warning us like a soothsayer
with veiled words about Odysseus,
I hear you, and I have something to say.
Let him come; now that strong
wine has given me courage,
I wrap my mind around his wife's softness.
My eyes, blinded by light, close
and carry away her nudity to Hades.

PHEMIOS

We're lost! Athena moves unhurriedly,
and in a single stride has reached the door.

EURYMACHOS

Get out, you fainthearted race of bards.

Odysseus: A Verse Tragedy

PHEMIOS

Yes, by all means, let me go before the doors slam shut
and the walls collapse.

TELEMACHOS

(*Blocking his path.*)

        Where do you think you're going?

ODYSSEUS

Let the loud mouth go; he can leave!
Double bar the doors
and stay alert; I'm going to signal soon.

KTESIPPOS

Onward, lads, make room for me.
I'm going to be the first to bend the bow.
Many times, the laurel crown
has adorned my curly head.
I've clipped the wings of Victory before.

ANTINOOS

You talk too much, bigmouth, clam up;
the twelve ax heads are waiting
and here is the massive bow; use it!

Nikos Kazantzakis

EUMAEUS

(Goes near the outer door where beggar/Odysseus is standing.)

What are you staring at? You too must be overjoyed
at my lady's wedding ...

ODYSSEUS

    Eumaeus,
my dog recognized me,
but not you my faithful servant!

EUMAEUS

    Oh my, whose voice is that?

ODYSSEUS

Don't shout; move aside, swineherd.
I didn't return to my neglected palace
to die but to kill.
Look into my eyes, look at the scar
on my thigh; remember? I'm Odysseus!

(Eumaeus scrambles to kiss his feet, but Odysseus restrains him.)

No, no, my faithful swineherd! We have neither
time to laugh nor cry.
Hold back your feelings and listen.

Odysseus: A Verse Tragedy

Close off the upper and lower floors
and remove the arms from the walls.
If anyone asks why you're taking them down, say,
"I'm afraid you might all get drunk
and embroil the wedding in blood."
When I signal, bring me the bow;
you on my left, my son on the right,
and sit tight; bright-eyed Athena leads.

PENELOPE

(*To herself, looking fearfully at beggar/Odysseus.*)

Good God, who might that be in our courtyard.
His penetrating look bores into my eyes.

(*Eumaeus secretly removes the arms from the walls. Ktesippos in vain struggles to bend the bow; the suitors laugh at him.*)

EURYMACHOS

Hey Ktesippos, why rack your brain
in vain and swelter?
Leave the bow to your superiors.
Your hairy thighs will not delight
in this victory's honeypot!

(*He takes the bow from him.*)

Nikos Kazantzakis

KTESIPPOS

Zeus, grant that neither will he enjoy
Penelope's breasts.

PENELOPE

It's beneath you
to fling evil spells on your betters.
Eurymachos, you should recall how
my husband took hold of the bow in his hands.
Slowly he drew his right arm back,
taut and tight like a bull's thigh,
until it gently touched flesh at his shoulder.
And what force his dark chest dispatched,
instantaneous without sweating.
Secretly, clenching his teeth,
the lightning-fast twanging arrow
flew with ease like a ravenous crow
as it passed through all twelve ax heads.

EURYMACHOS

You pursue us like virgin Artemis
dispatching hunting dogs after prey.
May procuress Aphrodite endow me
with children from your ample bosom
that one day I may be worthy to lay
deep roots in you for my descendants.

(*To the statue of Aphrodite.*)

Odysseus: A Verse Tragedy

You smile, almighty Aphrodite,
to see earth's living creatures
tremble in your delicate hands?
Men's teeth sink their passionate imprint
deep on your nape.
Select the best among us,
goddess of many men, who lurks in darkness.
Arise, shake off lust
and reward the best
in excellence, in reason, and in birth.

PENELOPE

Eurymachos, I like how wisely
you meld desire with right.
Now I lean over your shoulder
and counsel you willingly
not to waste time; kneel and draw
through the twelve ax heads, and I'm yours.

(Eurymachos tries in vain to bend the bow.)

ANTINOOS

You too are feeble; you sweat in vain.
Penelope's flattery has undone you.

PENELOPE

Offer fat bulls to Aphrodite.

Nikos Kazantzakis

ANTINOOS

To Ares also.

EURYMACHOS

   I can't do it; my arms
and thighs are spent…

PENELOPE

        Don't give up
Eurymachos … Come on, bite your lip,
be pig-headed and shoot.
As I recollect, he'd get a good grip
and at once it would fly like a swallow.
I don't expect a lesser husband.

EURYMACHOS

But I can't do it!

PENELOPE

       How disgraceful.

EURYMACHOS

          Penelope!

Odysseus: A Verse Tragedy

PENELOPE

Why holler? If you can't bend it, give it
to someone who can.

EURYMACHOS

    Here, Antinoos, take it.
I'm deeply hurt that it wasn't in the cards
for me to mount your ample
bed; but what irks me
even more: I'm not the man
Odysseus is, and in the generations to come
my humiliation will be everlasting.

PENELOPE

You were the one I favored
in heart and mind; but no longer will I escape
the arms of handsome Antinoos.

    (Laertes enters *from the outer door, alone, alert and erect.*)

EUMAEUS

Laertes!

PENELOPE

    Lovingly, I receive you father.

Nikos Kazantzakis

Welcome again to your palace;
to what do we owe the pleasure?

LAERTES

But didn't you send for me, my child?

PENELOPE

I did?

LAERTES

    Didn't you send a blue-eyed maiden for me,
who had an olive wreath in her hair?

PENELOPE

No, father, I didn't send anyone for you,
but you're more than welcome now that you're here.
Bring out the high chair, maids.

(*Addressing beggar/Odysseus.*)

Move, old timer, help him on the chair.
I'm grateful to whomever with a lie
welcomes you to the palace.

LAERTES

A gentle breeze brings

Odysseus: A Verse Tragedy

my heart back to life.
A heavenly virgin, a maiden
like a queen gently took me
by the hand and spoke in such
a delicate soft voice that soothed my mind,
and a tranquil light assailed my being.
"Grandfather they await you at the palace,
and I will lead you by the hand
until your elderly body of its own accord rejuvenates
by the time you arrive and sit upon your throne."
And I, leaning on her all-white shoulder,
took to the road step by step and sensed
such nimbleness that I thought
my feet had sprouted wings.
As I moved along, the fresh air
shed light on everything and confusion
melted in the sun like morning mist.

EUMAEUS

His mind is back. How alert
his speech and eyes are once again.
Miracles have their source.
It is clear that some god accompanied
him here.

ODYSSEUS

    Athena, I discern your spotless
hand giving his feet support
and enlightening my father's mind.

Nikos Kazantzakis

Such unparalleled goodness I never
hoped to see.

PENELOPE *(To herself.)*

      I'm afraid; a trembling
comes over me; you'd think a god is passing
silently like an eagle in flight.

ANTINOOS

Hey, maids, fetch me my golden cup;
suddenly, my heart missed a beat,
as if some wing brushed against my shoulder.
And you, why do you shuffle about like a thief
with sidelong glances and chatter incessantly?

LEODES

Brothers, the air grows thick.
An oppressive shadow stands before the door—
bring wine to calm our nerves.

KTESIPPOS

Hey, swineherd, why are you hiding our arms?

EUMAEUS

I'm afraid if you get drunk
you'll cause a bloodbath.

Odysseus: A Verse Tragedy

TELEMACHOS

Bring wine, fill the glasses.
Ktesippos, let the swineherd be
and drink to the new groom-to-be.

ANTINOOS

                         A toast
for this grubby beggar too... Today,
I want to shine even among the lowest of the low,
that like the sun with unvarying
brilliant intensity illuminates the earth.
And you good Aphrodite, who inflates
men's hunger with lustful apples
and inflames adolescent thighs,
come with a smile and loosen
fair Penelope's chastity belt.
Shake not your gloomy head
old beggar! Lift your cup
and drink a toast to Aphrodite.

ODYSSEUS

Which Aphrodite? Know
that my mind is not preoccupied with Cyprus's maidens
nor bed's pleasures; other gods
hold sway over me.

(*He performs a libation.*)

Nikos Kazantzakis

     Athena,
I call on you, indomitable virgin,
who soars full grown from the head
of humanity's creator like an all embracing
fire, wisdom, and strength.

(*Suddenly, a great flame emerges from Athena's altar.*)

LEODES

Good Heavens, a flame loomed up
from the Arbiter Athena's unlit altar.

ANTINOOS

Quickly throw wine on it and put it out.

TELEMACHOS

The goddess has entered my courtyard;
Don't anyone touch that flame.

PENELOPE

     My god,
I feel a net flung around me,
and I believe I detect the fisherman.

LAERTES

Maids, bring my ancestral cup,

Odysseus: A Verse Tragedy

fill it with wine and pay attention;
it's time for the grandfather to offer greetings.
Modest goddess, again a thousand times
welcome to my polluted home.
I pour three drops of black wine on the earth:
first for the grandfather, another for the absent son,
a third for the youthful grandson, and I shout
to my dead ancestors, who have shriveled from thirst,
and to my family roots thriving within the earth,
"open wide your mouths and drink."

TELEMACHOS

Act quickly, no time to lose. Fate
passes hurriedly through my courtyard,
entirely out of patience, and yells!

(*To Antinoos.*)

Hey braggart, don't take so long;
take your turn, muscleman; Fate's
footsteps are getting louder on the flagstones.

ANTINOOS

Ok. No need to shout. I'm in a hurry also,
to get into your mother's bed.
Oh, Fate, inclined toward courageous men,
come to me now with a victor's wreath;
the rest of you stand against the wall, I'm taking aim.

Nikos Kazantzakis

(He kneels and takes the bow, but he can't bend it. He jumps up angry and looks around.)

Who's laughing? Who's hissing like a snake?

(To beggar/Odysseus.)

Don't look at me! You jinx me,
you old geezer! Why are the doors bolted?
Open them, open up, I need air. I'm furious.

(To Telemachos.)

And you, why are you armed?

TELEMACHOS

                    The wine
has gone to your head and made you giddy;
put down the massive bow.
Mother, don't stand around
so many drunks. It's time you visit
Athena's idle altar in reverence
and rekindle its fading flame.
Tonight, for her, I sacrifice a hecatomb.

Any of you great men
worthy of filling Odysseus's bed
remain where you are; the gods keep their word.
The wedding tables will not be stripped.
Eurycleia, and the rest of you women, quickly,

Odysseus: A Verse Tragedy

I order you, retire upstairs
and should you hear cries, keep
the doors locked; the men alone
will handle what transpires.
                Master
of the house, stay seated upon your high throne.
Custodian of our home and
our family's source, like Zeus bless your son
and grandson from your lofty throne.

ODYSSEUS

Telemachos, I believe it's proper
for the revered queen to stay.
I'll press the gods to confirm
that the fated wedding take place.
One more suitor remains; have
patience lady, I beg you.

TELEMACHOS

Proceed, master of the house, your turn has come.

PENELOPE

My heart aches, something strange is going on.

(*Antinoos tries again to bend the bow but in vain.*)

ANTINOOS

I can't do it; someone has cursed me.
You, Penelope, were fated to remain abandoned
in your solitary bed lamenting,
but don't cry; a thousand other ways are known
to the benevolent goddess, and she will unite us.

(*The bow drops from Antinoos's hands; Eumaeus picks it up.*)

Leave the bow alone; bring it back!

TELEMACHOS

I'm the householder; I give the orders:
Shepherd, hand the bow to the old timer
that he may evoke his youth.

(*Beggar/Odysseus grabs the bow, releases the bowstring, which hums like a swallow. He signals Eumaeus and Telemachos standing on each side of him. He throws off his rags and blazes like a god.*)

LAERTES AND PENELOPE

Odysseus!

ODYSSEUS

Welcome fine gentlemen; where are you off to?
The doors are bolted. Bridegrooms,

Odysseus: A Verse Tragedy

the wedding in my wide courtyard is ready to begin.
Wife, hide in a corner,
in the chaos of slaughter an arrow—
be mindful lady—might injure you.
I'm Odysseus; my trusty bow
recognizes me, and in my hands, it longs for action.
Exultingly, the bowstring hums like a swallow.
In my ponderous hands, death brings
peace like a thunderbolt in the hand of justice.

been the recipient of seven awards from the Council of Editors of Learned Journals including the Phoenix Award for distinguished editorial achievement. Professor Myrsiades was also co-editor of the *Journal of the Hellenic Diaspora* (1991-2010), one of the leading journals in Neohellenic studies.

About the Translator

Kostas Myrsiades, Professor Emeritus of Comparative and Greek literature at West Chester University, is a distinguished translator and Neohellenist and the first American to receive the Gold Medallion (1995) for his translations from the Hellenic Society of Translators of Literature given annually by the Greek society to a scholar from any country. His work in Greek letters is demonstrated in his 24 published books and numerous articles and translations on modern and ancient Greek literature, among them his two volume readings of Homer's *Iliad* and *Odyssey* (Bucknell University Press, 2019-2022), his many book length translations of Yannis Ritsos and Takis Papatsonis co-translated with Kimon Friar, and his translations and studies of Karaghiozis, Greek shadow puppet theater co-authored with Linda Myrsiades. He has delivered many invited lectures for such groups as the Jane Globus Seminar Series at Baruch College, the Elytis Chair Lecture Series of Poetry and Neohellenic Studies at Rutgers University, and the Embassy of Greece/National Library of Canada at Ottawa. For twenty-two years, he served as editor of *College Literature*, a quarterly of literary criticism, theory, and pedagogy (1990-2012), which since 1990 has en were written in verse), three philosophical studies on Nietzsche, Bergson, and himself, a series of travel books (Greece, Spain, England, China, Japan, Israel, and Russia), and two books of poetry, *Terza Rima* and his monumental epic of 33, 333 verses, *Odyssey*, translated into English as *The Odyssey, A Modern Sequel* by Kimon Friar. He also wrote hundreds of articles for newspapers and encyclopedias, dozens of texts for Greek public schools, and numerous translations into modern Greek, among them Homer's *Iliad* and *Odyssey*, Dante's *Divine Comedy*, Goethe's *Faust, Part I*, Nietzsche's *Birth of Tragedy*, Bergson's *On Laughter*, and Darwin's *The Origin of Species*.

About The Author

Nikos Kazantzakis (1883-1957), the best known of modern Greek writers, was born in Crete and was twice nominated for the Nobel Prize in Literature. He studied at the University of Athens, where he received his Doctor of Laws degree, and later studied in Paris under the philosopher Henri Bergson. He served as Minister of Education of Greece (1945) and president of the Greek Society of Men of Letters. He traveled extensively through Germany, Italy, and Russia. Before World War II he spent most of his time on the island of Aegina devoting his time to his philosophical and literary work; his later years were spent in France. He died in Freiburg, Germany, in October 1957.

His major work, *Odyssey*, has been described as the single most ambitious literary accomplishment of the twentieth century. John Steinbeck recognized him as "one of the greatest writers of the twentieth century," and he was acclaimed by Albert Schweitzer, Thomas Mann, and world critics as one of the most eminent writers of our time. His oeuvre consists of thirteen novels, including *Zorba the Greek* and *The Last Temptation of Christ* (both of which were adapted into major feature films), eighteen dramatic works (of which sev-

Literary and Poetry Books from Somerset Hall Press

Dimitrios Bafaloukos, *Avaton: Poems*, translated by Vassiliki Rapti.

Deahn Berrini, *Milkweed*. A novel about a community coping with a beloved son returning from war.

Deahn Berrini, *A Roanoke Story*. Historical fiction about the first encounters between the Native people and the English settlers in North America from a Native perspective.

Euripides, *The Bacchae*, translated by Robert Zaller.

Lili Bita, *Fleshfire: Love Poems*.

Lili Bita, *Sister of Darkness: A Memoir*. The powerful story of a woman's journey of self-discovery and personal liberation.

Lili Bita, *The Storm Rider: A Memoir*. A story of intense maternal love for her son, and grief for his loss.

Lili Bita and Robert Zaller, trans., *Thirty Years in the Rain: The Selected Poetry of Nikiforos Vrettakos*. Poems by one of the most celebrated twentieth-century Greek poets.

Lili Bita, *The Thrust of the Blade: Poems*.

Lili Bita, *Women of Fire and Blood: Poems*. A feminist reimagining of the women of antiquity.

Tanya Contos, *The Tide Clock and other Poems*.

Roger Finch, *Stations of the Sun*. Poems inspired by life and travels in Asia.

Penelope Karageorge, *The Neon Suitcase: Poems*.

Dean Kostos, ed., *Pomegranate Seeds: An Anthology of Greek-American Poetry*.

Dean Papademetriou, ed., *Golden Anthology: Writings of a Greek-American Soldier in Korea*. Poems and stories by a Greek immigrant who was killed while heroically serving in the United States Army in Korea.

Shinjo: Reflections. Thoughts and sayings of a Buddhist master.

Soloúp, Aivali: A Story of Greeks and Turks in 1922, a graphic novel translated by Tom Papademetriou.

Stelios Ramfos, *Fate and Ambiguity in Oedipus the King*, translated by Norman Russell. A literary and philosophical reflection on the world-famous play, with a Foreword by renowned actor Olympia Dukakis.

Vassiliki Rapti, *Transitorium: Poems*.

Nanos Valaoritis, *Nightfall Hotel: A Surrealist Romeo and Juliet*, translated by Vassiliki Rapti.

Robert Zaller, *Islands*. Poems inspired by the Greek islands.

For more information about these books, including how to order them, please visit www.somersethallpress.com.